LILL
JEN
20
FORTUNE &
FENG SHUI
HORSE

KONSEPBOOKS
ASTROLOGY . FENG SHUI . INSPIRATIONS

Congratulations!

Hi there!

Firstly, I want to thank and congratulate you for investing in yourself… and the latest edition of Fortune and Feng Shui… your personalized horoscope book for 2012! Today you have purchased one of the best possible books on the market today to guide and help you safely through the upcoming year!

What will you be earning one year from today? How will you look and feel… will you be happier and healthier in 2012?

In this little book, Jennifer and I reveal many insights pertaining to your particular animal sign…what you can expect and how to protect and enhance all areas of your life for success in 2012.

But Why Stop Here?

Now you can discover other powerful feng shui secrets from me that go hand-in-hand with the valuable information in this book. And it's absolutely FREE!

My Personal Invitation

I'd like to extend my personal invitation to you to receive my FREE online weekly newsletter… Lillian Too's Mandala Ezine. You took the first positive step to success when you purchased this book. Now you can expand your wealth luck and knowledge…and learn more about authentic feng shui that really works… including the all-important 3rd dimension of spiritual feng shui when you sign up for my FREE newsletter.

Just go to *www.liliantoomandalaezine.com* and register today! My ezine will be delivered to your inbox each week loaded with great feng shui articles, hints and tips to make 2012 your best year ever.

IT'S EASY! IT'S FREE! IT'S FRESH AND NEW EACH WEEK!

Don't miss out! It's easy to register at *www.lilliantoomandalaezine.com* and you'll also receive a special BONUS from me when you register today!

All the best,
Lillian

P.S. Lillian's online FREE weekly ezine is only available to those who register online at *www.lilliantoomandalaezine.com*

P.P.S. Ezine subscribers also receive special offer, discounts and bonuses from me throughout the year!

Fortune & Feng Shui 2012 HORSE
by Lillian Too and Jennifer Too
© 2012 Konsep Lagenda Sdn Bhd

Text © 2012 Lillian Too and Jennifer Too
Photographs and illustrations © WOFS.com Sdn Bhd

The moral right of the authors to be identified as authors of this book has been asserted.

Published by KONSEP LAGENDA SDN BHD (223 855)
Kuala Lumpur 59100 Malaysia

For more Konsep books, go to www.lillian-too.com or www.wofs.com
To report errors, please send a note to errors@konsepbooks.com
For general feedback, email feedback@konsepbooks.com

Notice of Rights
All rights reserved. No part of this publication may be reproduced, stored in a retrieval system or transmitted in any form, or by any means, electronic, mechanical, photocopying, recording, or otherwise, without the prior written permission of the publisher.
For information on getting permission for reprints and excerpts, contact: permissions@konsepbooks.com

Notice of Liability
The information in this book is distributed on an "As Is" basis, without warranty. While every precaution has been taken in the preparation of the book, neither the author nor Konsep Lagenda shall have any liability to any person or entity with respect to any loss or damage caused or alleged to be caused directly or indirectly by the instructions contained in this book.

ISBN 978-967-329-079-6
Published in Malaysia, August 2011

for more on all the recommended
feng shui cures, remedies & enhancers for

2012

please log on to

www.wofs.com

and

www.fsmegamall.com

HORSE BORN CHART

BIRTH YEAR	WESTERN CALENDAR DATES	AGE	KUA NUMBER MALES	KUA NUMBER FEMALES
Metal Horse	30 Jan 1930 to 16 Feb 1931	82	7 West Group	8 West Group
Water Horse	15 Feb 1942 to 4 Feb 1943	70	4 East Group	2 West Group
Wood Horse	3 Feb 1954 to 23 Jan 1955	58	1 East Group	5 West Group
Fire Horse	21 Jan 1966 to 8 Feb 1967	46	7 West Group	8 West Group
Earth Horse	7 Feb 1978 to 27 Jan 1979	34	4 East Group	2 West Group
Metal Horse	27 Jan 1990 to 14 Feb 1991	22	1 East Group	5 West Group
Water Horse	12 Feb 2002 to 31 Jan 2003	10	7 West Group	8 West Group

CONTENTS

CHAPTER 1.
Dragon Year 2012 - General Outlook

Transformational Energies
Bring a Year of Far-reaching Changes   12
- The Year's Dominant Energies   12
- General Outlook for the year   21
- The PAHT CHEE chart of 2012   27
- Influence of the PAHT CHEE "stars"   35
- The FLYING STAR Numbers of 2012   41
- The "luck stars" of the 24 Mountains   60

CHAPTER 2.
Luck Of The Horse In 2012

Fortune Prospects & Energy Strength   77
- Outlook for the Lady Horse   88
- Outlook for the Gentleman Horse   92
- Energy Strength Analysis of Horse Luck in 2012   94
- Horse's Life Force & Health Luck   95
- Horse's Finance & Success Luck   96
- Horse's Chi Essence   98
- Water Horse – 70 & 10 yrs – Superb health luck   100
- Wood Horse – 58 yrs – Soften your stance to win   100
- Fire Horse – 46 yrs – Financial luck shines brightly   101
- Earth Horse – 34 yrs – Perseverance brings recognition   101
- Metal Horse – 22 yrs – Moving forward steadily & surely   102

CHAPTER 3.
Personalising Your Feng Shui Luck In 2012

Individualised Directions to Protect Your Good Feng Shui   103
- Making Horse's South 2 location auspicious   106
- Enhancing Horse's Personal Lo Shu Numbers   109
- Finetuning Auspicious Directions for Horse women   113
- Finetuning Auspicious Directions for Horse men   115
- Important pointers for work, health, study luck & relationships   116

CHAPTER 4.
Relationship Luck For 2012

The Horse's Popularity Soars with Friends and Colleagues Alike   125
- **Horse & Horse** – Competitive with each other   139
- **Horse With Tiger** – A great year for this pair of allies   141
- **Horse & Dog** – Allies yes, but divergent interests this year   143
- **Horse & Sheep** – Strong ties marred by hostility   148
- **Horse With Rat** – Strong potency in arrows of antagonism   153
- **Horse With Ox** – Overflowing with abundance - Sum of 10   157
- **Horse & Rabbit** – Too much loving so need to cool things   160
- **Horse & Dragon** – Good bonding goes beyond hand holding   162
- **Horse & Snake** – Keeping each other warm to stay loving   164
- **Horse & Monkey** – A subdued relationship this year   167
- **Horse & Rooster** – Flying high and making waves together   170
- **Horse & Boar** – Very little affinity between this pair   172

CHAPTER 5.
Analysing Your Luck In Each Month

Many months of the year favor you; but it is vital not to loosen your guard	174
February 2012 – Sum-of-ten brings luck.	175
March 2012 – Auspicious feng shui winds continue.	178
April 2012 – Be alert to fair weather friends.	181
May 2012 – Good fortune still smiling on you	184
June 2012 – Pressures bring misfortune	187
July 2012 – Back to the drawing board	190
August 2012 – Misunderstandings bring tensions	193
September 2012 – Autumn winds bring the sniffles	196
October 2012 – A month of double victory luck	199
November 2012 – Back on track once again	202
December 2012 – Extremely auspicious month	205
January 2013 – Be careful as you could get cheated	208

CHAPTER 6.
Powerful Protection Of Your Luck With Tien Ti Ren

Activating The Complete Trinity Of Luck With Spiritual Feng Shui   211

- **Special Incense Offerings** to appease local guardian spirits   218
- **Customized Tortoise Amulet** to strengthen Victory Luck   222
- **Clear Crystal Ball** to enhance Horse's recognition luck   225
- **Wish-Granting Gem Tree** for prosperity creation   226
- **Golden Wealth Wheel** Powerful Symbol of wealth creation   228
- **Plaque of Single Victory Horse** for winning luck   229
- **Fire Totem Talisman Pendant** to safeguard longterm luck   229
- **Guardian Bodhisattva** - Invoking Horse's Guardian Mahas-thama-Prapta   233

CHAPTER 1 : **DRAGON YEAR 2012**

YEAR OF THE WATER DRAGON 2012
A Transformational Year

In this new Year of the Water Dragon, the energy is colored by the powerful presence and strength of the Dragon, the Zodiac system's most powerful sign.

The year 2012 will be a transformational year, with Dragon energy permeating both positive and negative manifestations of luck, and for the Horse, the sign that sits on the Three Killings stars this year, Dragon energy brings much needed yang chi to propel it to new levels of victory and success.

But the Horse's inclinations this year blends well with the stars of the year's paht chee chart. The element relationships in the year's chart indicate that what is in store for everyone is far reaching and life changing, and for the Horse these changes will open new directions for you to pursue.

Dragon energy brings interesting challenges to you and for those in your prime, it could you get your adrenalin moving making you want to seek out new pastures and fresh worlds to conquer. Happily, this Dragon Year should illuminate your hidden talents, bringing out the independence of your spirit and the creativity of your instincts. The Horse will blend well with the energies of the new year!

However, first note the three stars influencing the energy of the year.

The *Star of Aggressive Sword* makes an appearance, so there is a great need to be wary. Violence in the world has not abated. There continues to be an air of collective anger pervading the world's atmosphere, which continues to find an outlet.

Interestingly also, in the 2012 paht chee chart, the Tiger (who is the Horse's ally) continues to be around and it is a strong Water Tiger who complements the year's Water Dragon. With Tiger and Dragon present in the chart, and the Rooster as well (which symbolizes the Phoenix and is the Dragon's secret friend), we see the presence of three celestial guardians as well as the powerful hand of heaven.

It is a year when destinies play out with brutal efficiency and big transformations take place. This is

CHAPTER 1 : DRAGON YEAR 2012

confirmed by the number 6 in the center of the feng shui chart. Heavenly energies rule this year. Cosmic forces are extremely powerful in 2012 and the best way to ride the Dragon Year, the most effective way to emerge stronger and healthier, happier and richer this year, is to rely greatly on powerful cosmic guardians. And to always wear symbols of victory!

With your ally in the chart, you should also suit yourself up with your Crest of Allies. This attracts victory luck as nothing else can, and for you, victory in all that you do gets a big boost from the year's feng shui winds! But note that to enjoy your victory luck, you need to stay safe always, and in a year like 2012, you need protection.

Indeed, it is a year when protection and enhancers are important aides to riding the Dragon Year. It is thus beneficial to learn subduing rituals that ward off bad luck, and also to have powerful symbols of protection and enhancement in the home.

It is a year when wearing protective powerful mantras and syllables on the body can be the difference between sailing through the year safely or becoming some kind of victim.

Protective amulets should always be worn touching the energy vortexes of the throat, the heart and also near to the navel where the body's central chakra is located and where all the "winds" of the body's channels converge. Strengthening the chakras of the human body system enhances attunement to the environment. We are currently living through a time when the energies of the world are in a state of flux. Staying protected and in sync with the disturbing energies of the environment is not difficult and is worth the small effort involved.

> The Dragon Year brings also the star of *External Flower of Romance*, a star which fuels potentially painful passions. Those hit by it and engage in affairs out of wedlock are certain to create hurtful waves and aggravations in their lives! Relationship woes could well escalate in 2012; it will be worse than last year and no one is immune.

It is wise to take some strong precautions. Bring good feng shui protection into the bedroom and be particularly conscious of auspicious sleeping directions that protect the family and your marriage relationship this year. Also put into place safeguards that protect your particular love relationship.

For the ambitious and those determined to succeed, the year also brings the *Star of Powerful Mentors*. For the younger generation of Horse i.e. the **22 year old Metal Horse** you need mentor help to put you onto the path of success.

Activate the year's mentor luck energy by energizing the Northwest of your room with a **Kuan Kung** image. Being on the receiving end of mentor luck brings the auspicious support of influential people entering your life to give you a helping hand.

Mentors will open doors to great careers and to those still in University or College, mentors also help win scholarships and further education opportunities.

For everyone born in the Horse Year, do note that the presence of Fire in your personal chart is most helpful because as a Horse, you are intrinsically Fire! The Fire element brings you a better balanced set of energies to be in sync with the year. There will therefore be unseen hands supporting all Horse-born people.

CHAPTER 1 : **DRAGON YEAR 2012**

Compass directions and locations of sleeping areas must be correctly monitored this year; and the symbol of the Crystal Globe with a Dragon perched at the top ascending towards the Universe & the skies attracts the all-important heaven luck.

The Crystal Globe with Dragon attracts all-important heaven luck this year.

We have designed a very special crystal globe to be placed in the center of homes especially for this purpose - to act as a catalyst. This Dragon on a Crystal Globe adds much towards enhancing the energy of the Horse's home and office as this is what will pull in the much-needed heaven luck into your space.

CHAPTER 1 : DRAGON YEAR 2012

You should also take note of the luck of different months so that your luck is properly fine-tuned. Know your good months, for these are times when you can be confident and when opportunities will ripen in an auspicious manner. Troubled months are when it is advisable to refrain from making big decisions or embarking on important journeys. They are also the times to put suitable remedies in place so that whatever setbacks, illnesses or disappointments that make an appearance will be minor in nature.

This series of *Fortune & Feng Shui books* for the 12 animal signs of the Lunar Zodiac is written based on studies made into the year's Paht Chee and feng shui charts. Information in these charts are combined with Flying Star feng shui technology, 24 Mountains Compass Stars cycle and the Tibetan Wheel of Elements to bring you accurate readings on what to expect for the coming year.

But these books are not merely passive readings of luck. We go to great lengths to analyze the charts and research the cures so that we can incorporate powerful feng shui and astrological recommendations. Our philosophy of practice is that bad luck should always be effectively averted and good luck must always be strongly activated to manifest.

CHAPTER 1 : DRAGON YEAR 2012

This year we bring focus to house layout recommendations and feng shui directions as these appear to offer the best ways of taking fullest advantage of the Dragon, Tiger and Phoenix celestial presence in the paht chee chart. This is an auspicious configuration which has the potential to channel heavenly good fortune your way.

So included within is advice about placement of symbolic objects that have a celestial connection. Placed correctly within the home, they act as catalysts to luck, thus facilitating your journey through the year, ensuring you sail through relatively trouble free.

The big thing for 2012 is the power of the Blue Dragon and the great importance of Fire energy, because Fire is missing in this year's chart. The presence of Fire will instantly improve the luck of any space. So, this year, do invest in bright lights.

The presence of **crystal/glass globes** and **wishgranting jewels** in the center of the home will also be especially auspicious, as these bring the luck of increasing wealth. In 2012, the element that signifies prosperity is the Earth element, so having crystal balls on your coffee tables, especially those embellished with auspicious symbols and important sutras, are sure to offer excellent harmonious relationship luck as well as prosperity luck.

In 2012, the element that signifies Prosperity is the Earth element.

> These books are meant to assist readers to understand how their astrological and destiny luck can be improved with good feng shui in this important transformational year of the Dragon. Recommendations are based on calculations and interpretations of the charts, and analysis has been simplified so that the advice given is easily understood. Even those with no previous experience with feng shui or fortune enhancement practices will find it easy, fun and ultimately very effective using astrology and the placement of symbolic objects to improve their luck.

This book on the Horse's fortunes for 2012 is one of twelve written specially for each Zodiac sign. It offers almost a recipe-type, easy approach to preparing for the year ahead. If you find it helpful for yourself, you might also want to monitor the luck pattern of your loved ones. Who knows how good advice given within may be just the thing to jump start their auspicious fortune, causing it to ripen!

This is a year when everything good or bad will seem to be larger than usual in magnitude and definitely transformational in effect. It is worthwhile taking some trouble to ensure that the year's energy really does sync beautifully with yours.

GENERAL OUTLOOK FOR THE YEAR

The world witnessed a record number of earthquakes, floods, storms, forest fires and volcanic eruptions in the past two years, creating a disaster-driven scenario which last year was compounded by the severity of violence and civil conflicts in many of the world's troubled countries.

The last two years 2010 and 2011 saw troubled times brought by the clash of stem and branch elements, not just in the important year pillar, but also in all the other pillars. These paht chee chart indications bring suffering and loss on a global scale, and in the immediate past year they manifested in different parts of the world with frightening reality. The violence that erupted in the countries of the Middle East was scary, but so were city shattering earthquakes, widespread floods, gigantic storms and volcanic eruptions, all of which started towards the closing months of 2011. These seem to lend credence to the highly publicized end of the world predictions for 2012.

Yet happily, amidst all the natural disasters and violence that have occurred, those who stayed safe also went on to enjoy good times and good news. This was because the year 2011 also benefited from powerful feng shui winds and enjoyed windows of good fortune brought by quite a good number of big and small auspicious star energies from the 24 mountain compass stars.

So although the destiny chart of elements of the past couple of years did bring turbulent times and conflicts to many parts of the world, these discordant energies told only half the story. On a micro basis many were able to seize the opportunities that manifested during the past year.

For 2012, Chinese Astrology does not predict an end of world scenario. But will we see an end to the disaster scenario of the past two years? The charts suggest so. 2012 is the year of the powerful Water Dragon, and the astrological indications of the year are predicting

CHAPTER 1 : DRAGON YEAR 2012

a transformational year. There are absolutely no signs of the physical world coming to an end, but the charts do point to a time of great upheavals brought about by the natural disasters of past years and also rather awesome change; the world as we know it will continue on a path of transformation started two years ago, and gathering momentum in 2012.

The changes are political as well as economic and they will impact the lives of many people and also change the balance of influence and power in the world. But the good news is that it is also a year of renewal - at least the beginnings of good times ahead - of seeing the light at the end of the tunnel.

The Dragon Year always symbolizes an apex of change. It is the celestial creature of Spring, so a year ruled by the Dragon is always a time when the world will experience new beginnings in multiple dimensions of existence.

The 2012 Dragon will see many countries changing directions in terms of allegiances and economic emphasis. New leaders will also emerge and violence could precede or follow upon such change. Commercially, the world becomes more competitive and demanding. Relationships are edgy and there is an absence of general goodwill. This is due to the preponderance of yearly conflict stars. And there is also the influential Aggressive Star hanging over the year's paht chee.

So although natural disasters and severe fallouts caused by weather changes reduce in severity, human conflicts continue to escalate. Tolerance among world leaders is almost nonexistent so we shall hear the rattling of threats and the smell of war.

This is compounded by the clashing elements in the year pillar of the Dragon - when Earth clashes with Water - so conflicts do not get resolved. Happily for mankind, this is not a fierce clash. Here, it is Earth stabilizing Water rather than Metal destroying Wood.

Besides, it is a year when the presence of the lap chun brings the promise of potentially good growth. When growth energy is as strong as it is in this new year, it brings a good harvest, so symbolically, this is a very encouraging sign. Also, there is ONE pillar of the paht chee chart that shows a productive relationship between the elements, that of Yang Water producing Yang Wood in the Month pillar. This gives hope of rejuvenation.

CHAPTER 1 : DRAGON YEAR 2012

The year also sees the heavenly lucky 6 in the center of the feng shui chart, and this brings auspicious luck from above. Engaging the energy of tien or heaven is the key to staying in perfect sync with the year, and is what will unlock good fortune. According to feng shui, this means inviting heavenly and cosmic Deities into the home.

It is interesting to note that according to many of the great Siddhics of India, 2012 is the start of the Age of Aquarius. We lived through the ending of the Age of Pisces last year, when we witnessed severe cataclysmic events and strong weather changes.

It is now the start of a spectacular period of Spiritual Revival when heavenly energy, which brings with it the magic of white yang energy bright to light up the world and get it ready to welcome the Period of 9 in 2024.

This is also a year blessed by the presence of three celestial creatures - the Dragon, Tiger and Phoenix (the presence of the Rooster in the year's chart signifies the phoenix) and these bring very welcome powerful and protective energies. Astrologically therefore, this is a much better year than last year in terms of planting new growth and reaping good harvests. The energies of the Dragon Year are conducive to new ideas and new ways of improving oneself. Investments can be made on healthy foundations and prosperity can be nurtured.

> **ENHANCER FOR THE YEAR:** To complete the quartet of celestial protectors it is extremely beneficial if there are tortoises in your home; either you keep live ones, or you at least have the images of these wonderfully auspicious creatures. If you believe in feng shui, you should have tortoises in your homes for they signify not just the protective energy of the Universe, they are also magnificent symbols of longevity.

THE PAHT CHEE CHART OF 2012

This is the Four Pillars chart of the year and reveals not just the general trends of the year but also gives a helicopter view of what can be expected in terms of trends and opportunities. The chart comprises the basket of eight elements that influence the luck of the year.

HOUR	DAY	MONTH	YEAR
HEAVENLY STEM	HEAVENLY STEM	HEAVENLY STEM	HEAVENLY STEM
乙	乙	壬	壬
YIN WOOD	YIN WOOD	YANG WATER	YANG WATER
EARTHLY BRANCH	EARTHLY BRANCH	EARTHLY BRANCH	EARTHLY BRANCH
辛酉	己未	甲寅	戊辰
METAL ROOSTER	EARTH SHEEP	WOOD TIGER	EARTH DRAGON

HIDDEN HEAVENLY STEMS OF THE YEAR

| - | YIN WOOD / YIN FIRE | YANG EARTH / YANG FIRE | YIN WATER / YIN WOOD |

THE YEAR IS DESPERATELY SHORT OF FIRE I.E. INTELLIGENCE & CREATIVITY

CHAPTER 1 : DRAGON YEAR 2012

The composition of this basket of elements - Fire, Earth, Metal, Water and Wood - and the frequency of their appearance in the chart - is what shows us what elements are missing, in short supply or in excess. Here is the Paht Chee chart of the year 2012. We also analyze the chart to determine the stability of the year's energies and go deeper too, to look for hidden elements that bring additional inputs to the year.

The 2012 chart has only four of the five elements, so it is incomplete. There is one element missing. The missing element is FIRE which suggests to anyone who understands the vital importance of balancing the elements that everyone's home will benefit from extra lighting during the coming year. Keeping the home well-lit instantly enhances the energies of any home, bringing a more auspicious foundation for the year.

It is beneficial to install more lights, keep curtains to a minimum and to literally bring the sunshine in. The Fire element in 2012 signifies intelligence and creativity, and there is a shortage of this during the year, so bringing well thought out ideas to any situation improves the success equation.

It is the clever and the wise who will ultimately prevail this year. So curb your impulses and always think things through before making important decisions.

Happily there are two hidden **Fire** elements in the chart and this makes up for the lack of Fire in the main chart. This is a good sign, but hidden Fire can also mean Fire erupting, so there will continue to be calamities associated with hidden Fire.

Wood Energy Too Strong

Meanwhile, looking deeper into the chart, we see that there is more than enough Wood and Water energy in 2012. In fact, Wood energy is very strong, and could even be too strong. This suggests a degree of competitiveness that can turn ugly; excess Wood makes everyone more combative and scheming than usual.

Neither friends nor allies are particularly helpful to each other. The hard-line impulses of the year's energies tend to be pervasive, so for the next twelve months, it is a case of every man for himself being the rallying cry. There is also very serious jostling for power and rank in many people's lives. Especially amongst leaders, people in charge, and those who supervise others… their motivation will mainly be to outdo and outperform whoever is identified as the challenger. Success this year has to be achieved against this very competitive scenario. It plays out on any scale, macro or micro, from the smallest office situation to the global world stage; in the playing fields or in the workplace.

The energy of the working world tends to be antagonistic and hostile, fueled by the presence of the *Aggressive Star*.

Words spoken will be louder and more forceful, and especially between those at the top. Amongst patriarchal people, many will tend to be extraterritorial, more assertive and very definitely more uncompromising. This attitude of belligerence will be the main obstacle to harmony this year.

Amongst the four pillars of the chart, you can see that three of them have clashing elements.

In the Year pillar, the heavenly stem of Yang Water clashes with the Earthly branch of Yang Earth. Here the heavenly stem energy is subdued by the earthly branch. The Dragon's earthly influence will be strong.

CHAPTER 1 : DRAGON YEAR 2012

In the Day pillar, the heavenly stem of Yin Wood destroys the Earthly branch of Yin Earth. Here, the heavenly stem prevails. The Sheep essence here is subdued by heavenly energy.

In the Hour pillar, the heavenly stem of Yin Wood is destroyed by the Earthly branch of Yin Metal. We see here the earthly strength of the Rooster.

> With 3 out of 4 of the pillars clashing, the year will not be peaceful. Harmony is a hard commodity to come by. But note that in the Month pillar, Yang Water enhances Yang Wood. This is very auspicious as this means there is growth energy during the year.

WEALTH LUCK IN 2012 is signified by the element of Earth and with two of these in the main chart as well as one hidden Earth element, there is wealth luck during the year. It should not be difficult for wealth luck to manifest or to get enhanced. What is great is that in the hidden elements of this Month pillar, we see the presence of Fire enhancing Earth.

This is a good sign and since it is the Month pillar, it benefits those who undertake wealth-enhancing activities during the months that are favorable for them. So do make an effort to remember your lucky months during the course of the year. Getting your timing right is often the key to making good decisions.

> **For the Horse person, the lucky months for engaging in prosperity-enhancing activities are February, March, May, October, November and December, so for you, half of the year looks very auspicious indeed.**

Note that these are the months when you will benefit from some excellent feng shui winds blowing your way, so you have to be prepared to take advantage. Be mindful this year to not get distracted!

RESOURCE LUCK IN 2012 is represented by the element of Water. There are two direct Water and one hidden Water in the chart and once again, this is a good sign as it means there will be enough resources to keep the year's growth energy stable and strong. In paht chee readings, emphasis is always placed on the stability of good luck manifesting. This year, Water ensures that the intrinsic Wood energy of the year is kept constantly nourished. The resource availability situation appears good. This also suggests that the price of oil will not be so high as to cause problems to world economic growth. The main danger is that there might be excess Water. Too much Water can create an imbalance, in which case it should be balanced by the presence of Fire energy. The clever balancing of elements in your living space is the key to attracting and sustaining good fortune, so make an effort to increase the presence of Fire energy in your living and working spaces.

Use red scatter cushions and red curtains, and enhance your lighting this year!

POWER LUCK IN 2012 is represented by the element of Metal and in the chart there is one occurrence of Metal represented by the earthly branch of the Rooster sign. That there is only a single occurrence of Metal suggests however that power luck in 2012 is not strong; that it is in the Hour pillar means power chi comes more towards the end of the year, and power this year is held by the young person.

The year favors power that is exercised by the younger generation of the family, and more effective when wielded by females.

What is very encouraging is that the Rooster and Dragon are secret friends of the Astrological Zodiac. The presence of this auspicious pair in the year's Paht Chee bodes well for the beginning and end of the year. Their joint presence also subdues to some extent the conflict energy of the year.

Presence of the 3 Celestial Protectors

The Dragon, Phoenix and Tiger appearing together in the chart is also another good indication. These are three of the four celestial guardians of any space. They signify that **protector energy** is present during the year and to make the energy complete, it is very beneficial in 2012 to invite in the celestial Tortoise.

In 2012, all homes benefit from the presence of the **Celestial Tortoise**. Inviting an image of the tortoise into the home is beneficial and timely. Better yet is to start keeping some live tortoises or terrapins. Doing so completes the powerful quartet of celestial guardians in your home.

INFLUENCE OF THE PAHT CHEE STARS

In 2012, we see the presence of three powerful stars in the Paht Chee chart. These bring additional dimensions to the year's outlook. They define the attitudes that have a dominant influence on people's tendencies and behavior. The three stars are:

- the Star of Aggressive Sword
- the Flower of External Romance
- the Star of Powerful Mentors

Star of Aggresive Sword

This star suggests a year of intensive aggression. It indicates the strengthening of the underdog's chi energy, so it does point to a continuation of the revolutionary energies started last year. Across the globe, there will be a rise of revolutionary fervor; people revolting against established authority.

At its zenith, the presence of this star suggests the emergence of powerful rebel leaders, or of highly influential opposition to established leaders. It suggests the emergence of people who seize power by fair means or foul. The name of this star is Yang Ren, which describes yang essence sharp blade that inflicts damage. This is a star that has great potential for either very good or very bad influences to materialize during the year, although generally, the influence tends to be more negative than positive. Unfortunately in the chart of this year, the Star of Aggressive Sword is created by the strong Yin Wood of the Day Pillar with the presence of the Tiger in the Month pillar.

Here, note that the Wood element is strong in the chart, making the presence of the Aggressive Sword Star much more negative. It indicates that those emerging as leaders for the underdog in 2012 will end up being heavy-handed and quick-tempered.

They are charismatic but will also be strong-willed, arrogant, overbearing and self-centered - all negative traits that spell potential for bloodshed and violence wherever they emerge. This is a real danger for the year!

> **CURE:** If you need protection against being hit by the *Star of Aggressive Sword*, or if you live in a part of the world where revolution has just occurred or where violence prevails, you will need the powerful **Earth Stupa of Protection**. This stupa is filled with powerful Dharmakaya Relic mantras and has a protective amulet on its façade which protects against dangers of any kind of violence around you.

CHAPTER 1 : DRAGON YEAR 2012

The Earth Stupa of Protection is the best cure to use to stay protected against the Star of Aggressive Sword this year.

Flower of Romance (External)

The *Flower of Romance* is sometimes confused with the *Peach Blossom Star* because it addresses the subject of love. When the flower of romance is present in the Eight Characters chart, it suggests that there is genuine love and caring between husband and wife.

But this is a star that also reveals the occurrence of extramarital affairs. The differentiation is made between internal romance and external romance, with the latter implying the occurrence of infidelity.

The Flower of Romance Star indicated in this year's chart is that of external romance, so it suggests the occurrence of infidelity within long term love relationships, causing problems and heartaches. Marriages suffer the dangers that this year's flower of romance star poses. It is thus really helpful to wear or display the safeguards that protect the sanctity of love relationships.

In 2012 the external flower of romance is created by the earthly branch Dragon in the Year pillar and the earthly branch Rooster in the Hour pillar.

CURE: To combat this serious affliction during the year, those of you worried about infidelity in your marriage or have cause to suspect your partner of harboring thoughts of infidelity, wear **the amulet which protects against third party interference** in your relationship (and this is very powerful) OR you can also invite in **the image of a Dog & Rabbit** to counter the affliction. This subdues the possibility of infidelity causing problems for you. The Dog/Rabbit presence will create a special "cross" with the Dragon/Rooster affliction in the year's chart.

Star of Powerful Mentors

Chinese Astrology makes much of "mentor" luck, and in the old days, having a powerful patron looking after your career path at the Emperor's court was an important success factor. The prospects facing young scholars hoping to rise to powerful positions at the Court of the Emperor was always enhanced with the help of someone influential.

In modern times, it is just as excellent to enjoy the luck of being supported, helped and guided by powerful benefactors. Indeed, success often comes from "who you know rather than what you know."

In 2012, the presence of the Star of Powerful Mentors emphasizes the importance of Mentor Luck, so that those having someone powerful to help them in their professional or business career will have the edge in terms of attaining success.

ENHANCER: To attract Mentor Luck, display a large statue of **Kuan Kung, the God of Advancement and Wealth**, in the front part of the home or in the Northwest corner of the home. The presence of this proud Taoist Deity is believed to attract into the home the powerful support of a patriarchal figure that will bring good influence to the lives of those about to embark on a career. Kuan Kung also protects against violence that may harm the patriarch!

FLYING STAR NUMBERS OF 2012

The Flying Star chart of 2012 is dominated by the auspicious heavenly star number 6 in the center. This is a strong star. It brings a multi-dimensional manifestation of unexpected good fortune, especially when it gets activated.

Activating any good flying star in any year is part of practising time dimension feng shui. There are three effective ways of putting this energy to work for you, all three of which are done with the intention of attracting yang chi into the part of the home which houses the auspicious "star number", in this case the number 6 in the center of the home or the center of any room.

The three methods of activating yang chi are:

Firstly, create noise...
with a radio or television placed here in the center.

Secondly, create activity...
by having a sitting arrangement here. Human energy is most powerful in activating the chi.

Thirdly, create light...

place a bright light in the place where the 6 is located. In 2012, this has a double benefit, as Fire energy represented by light is what brings excellent balancing feng shui.

When energized in any of these three ways, the number 6 will be activated to bring good energies into the home. It is also possible to enhance this star number further by placing powerful Earth element energy here in the center of the home.

The Earth element magnifies the power of metallic 6, so having crystal or glass balls on a coffee table in the center of your living room would be most auspicious. The best is to have at least a couple of crystal balls that have auspicious images or mantras lasered onto the crystal.

Remember that crystal is a very effective empowering medium and above all things, crystals bring harmony and a sense of loving kindness into the home. So this is something we recommend strongly. Crystals also empower Earth energy which in 2012 brings prosperity luck.

The feng shui benefits of displaying six smooth crystal balls in the home always brings harmony and enhances loving energies. In 2012, this is one thing that would be extremely beneficial to bear in mind.

> In 2012, it is a good idea to activate the Fire element inside the home, as this element, which represents intelligence and creativity, is missing from the feng shui chart. Enhancing the home with strengthened Fire will activate the good star numbers of the chart.

You can do this by introducing a red crystal ball placed amongst the rest of them on your coffee table. You can also add more light into the heart of your home - consider installing brighter light bulbs or bringing in white lampshades that create pockets of lit-up areas throughout your home. Also add extra light to the Southwest of the home. Adding to the brightness of the Southwest strongly enhances the matriarchal energy while subduing the hostile star number 3 which flies there in 2012. This will strengthen the mother energy of the home, which benefits the mother figure of the family and these benefits extend to the entire family.

CHAPTER 1 : DRAGON YEAR 2012

FLYING STAR CHART OF 2012

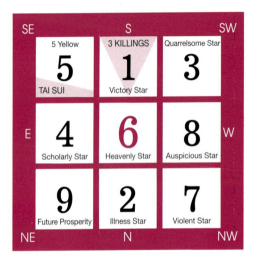

The chart shown here reveals how the nine numbers of the original Lo Shu square are laid out in the different sectors of the home for 2012. This is probably the best way to understand the feng shui pattern of the year, as it shows how energy congregates within any built-up structure. The nine numbers laid out as shown should be superimposed onto the layout plans of homes and offices in order to understand the luck of sectors, corners and rooms in the home or office.

> Every level of the home is affected by the chart, so it is necessary to superimpose the chart on every floor level of your home/office.

Each of the numbers carries energy which can be auspicious or unlucky. The numbers each have an intrinsic meaning which reflects luck patterns congregating in each of the different compass sectors of the home. Feng shui practitioners are familiar with all the afflictive and auspicious natures of the nine numbers; and lineage texts on feng shui offer specific ways of subduing the bad numbers and enhancing the lucky numbers.

This is basically how the feng shui of homes can be updated and improved each year. It is a method that has not failed, so each year, the updating procedures to ensure feng shui continues to be good requires the chart of the year to be analyzed and acted upon.

Enhancing the 6 in the Center

The most important thing to do first is to strengthen the center number 6, which is auspicious, and this we have already done by increasing lights in the center and displaying Earth element energy here with crystal balls or other auspicious images made of crystal.

If you can afford them, you can display crystal images that have genuine 24 carat gold embedded within. This is extremely lucky for everyone within the household and also attracts wealth luck for the family.

Strengthening the 1 in the South to Benefit the Horse

The victory star 1 flies to the South, bringing good fortune success luck to bedrooms located here in 2012. So if you sleep in such a room you will enjoy the luck of victory and success.

As someone born in the Horse year, it brings you double benefit if you also live in the South corner of your house or apartment i.e. if your bedroom is located in the South. You can also place the image of a beautiful **Victory Horse** here as this activates hidden powers of courage and endurance of this magnificent creature to the South.

Displaying the **Banner of Victory** in the South of the living area OR having a small water feature here are other excellent ways to cause the power energy in the home to manifest. This will be especially beneficial to the young women of the family - i.e. the daughters of the family.

Activating the 8 in the West

West sectors of their home will benefit from the powerfully potent number 8 star, which flies into this corner in 2012. Here, the auspicious effect of the 8 star is strongly magnified by the *Yi Duo Star* which has also flown here brought by the compass stars of the 24 Mountain directions.

The 8 star also benefits all those whose main entrance door into their homes are located in the West sector of their home. You can then enhance the foyer area of your home with brighter lighting as Fire enhances the earth element of the 8 star. You can also place a red crystal ball with sutra here or in your West-situated bedroom to activate the power of 8. Also try and keep the door opened as much as possible to let the energy of 8 flow in.

Note that using the Fire element to activate the 8 star also subdues the Metal element of the West. Metal weakens the Earth star 8, so having it subdued will enhance the balance in favor of the 8 star. The advice given here also benefits all those with offices located in the West part of their building.

Those looking for more things to display in the foyer to improve the auspiciousness of their abode can also place the liu li figure 8 here; or an image of the **Phoenix**. This not only activates the West sector but also the presence of the Rooster in the year's paht chee chart.

Good feng shui is very much about enhancing the energy patterns of the home, and placement of the correct symbols in the correct corners of the home does go a very long way towards doing this.

Place the Phoenix in the West sector this year to activate the auspicious star 8 here.

Nurturing the 4 in the East

Contrary to what some believe, the number 4 does not bring negative connotations or bad luck under the flying star system of feng shui, and in fact, this is the number most often associated with peach blossom or romance.

 MARRIAGE PROSPECTS: Feng shui traditionalists regard the number 4 as the number which enhances the opportunities of marriage within families whose main entrance doors face its location, and for those whose bedrooms are placed where it flies into for the year. In 2012, the number 4 flies to the East.

The element of the East is Wood, which is in harmony with the element of 4, which is also Wood. But the energy of the number 4 star is not strong. This is because it is also affected by the *Star of Reducing Energy* brought by the compass stars of the 24 mountains.

As such, it is advisable to strengthen the number 4 star with Water element energy here. Placing a **water feature** here is one way of doing this. So if your home is facing East, or if your main door is placed in the East sector of the home, having Water element energy here would be very helpful in activating the positive attributes of the 4 star.

CHAPTER 1 : DRAGON YEAR 2012

> **STUDY LUCK:** Note that the number 4 is also regarded as the scholarly star, bringing luck to all kinds of academic pursuits. If your family comprise children or teenagers still at school or in College, nurturing the number 4 star with a small water feature brings them good fortune luck to their studies, in their examinations and to their applications for admissions into reputable Colleges.

It is however worthwhile noting that the water features used must not be too big, otherwise the number 4 can turn ugly, bringing the affliction of infidelity and sexual scandal. So keep the presence of water here properly balanced.

A water feature in the East will strengthen the positive aspects of this flying star. Just ensure you do not install a water feature that is too big for your home, as this will overwhelm the home and create an imbalance.

Magnifying the 9 in the Northeast

This number represents future prosperity. It is also the magnifying and expanding number which expands both good and bad. Note that the intrinsic element of 9 is Fire, another reason it is so welcome here in the Northeast.

The Fire element enhances the sector's Earth element, strengthening the energy of this part of the house. If your bedroom is located here, you will enjoy all the benefits that the number 9 brings, including permanence to all the good luck you successfully build on.

If your door faces Northeast or is located in the Northeast of the home, it will be very beneficial to add lights to this sector at the start of the year. Enhance the lighting of the doorway area of the home both inside and outside. Doing so will magnify the long term luck prospects of the family.

The Horse-born living here in 2012 will successfully tap into the luck of the powerful 9, and since this is also the location of your ally the Tiger, it will be beneficial having your bedroom in this corner.

CHAPTER 1 : **DRAGON YEAR 2012**

> 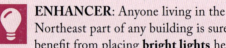 **ENHANCER**: Anyone living in the Northeast part of any building is sure to benefit from placing **bright lights** here. This will attract powerful yang chi and Fire energy, which ensures the sector benefits from the number 9 star here.

Subduing the Illness Star 2 in the North

In 2012 the illness star 2 flies to the North, bringing the sickness affliction to all those whose bedrooms are placed in the North of their homes. And if the front door is placed in the North sector, then the effect of this affliction affects everyone living within.

The illness star is an Earth element star, and happily, its flight into the North does not strengthen it, unlike last year when the illness star in the South brought a great deal of sickness to many people.

Nevertheless, it is a good idea to subdue this affliction as it is never pleasant getting sick or succumbing to the fever bug, the coughing bug or the flu bug.

CHAPTER 1 : DRAGON YEAR 2012

Worse, the illness star weakens the resistance of all those whose life force or chi energy is not strong.

The Horse-born does not have very strong Life Force luck or Chi Essence in 2012, so for you, the illness star 2 is quite formidable. It is thus better NOT to sleep in a North-located room, and if possible, do not enter or leave the house (or office) via a North facing or North located door in 2012.

In a month when your energy is being hit by the illness star, i.e. in September especially, you should avoid this sector altogether. If not you could get sick!

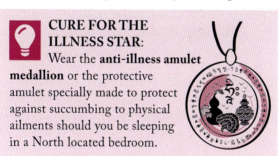

CURE FOR THE ILLNESS STAR: Wear the **anti-illness amulet medallion** or the protective amulet specially made to protect against succumbing to physical ailments should you be sleeping in a North located bedroom.

Suppressing Yellow Star 5 in the Southeast

Those familiar with feng shui afflictions know how awful the yellow star 5 can be. This is the star number that brings a whole series of bad news, illness, obstacles to success and all kinds of depressing feelings. It creates an aura of despondency and unhappiness and actually causes moods and attitudes to just go haywire.

It rarely surprises us when those affected by the 5 Yellow start being more sensitive than usual to imagined slights, or who become extra prone to finding faults with others.

In 2012, this affliction affects those whose bedrooms or whose main doors into their homes are situated on or facing the Southeast direction. The Horse must definitely be very mindful of this affliction, especially if your bedroom is located in this part of the house.

If you stay in a Southeast located room, your energy gets weakened and this is something that becomes quite excessive during the month of June when your own sector gets afflicted also by the 5 Yellow.

CHAPTER 1 : **DRAGON YEAR 2012**

> 💡 **CURE FOR THE FIVE YELLOW:**
> A good cure continues to be the **five element pagoda** embellished with the Tree of Life which we introduced last year. This pagoda continues to be a powerful remedy for this afflictive star.
>
> In this year of the Dragon however, it is also very beneficial to add the powerful seed syllables associated with purifying Fire energy, as this has the added advantage of engaging the spiritually powerful cures associated with these symbols.
>
> These are the syllables *Bam*, *Hrih* and *Ah* which are advised in the Tibetan astrological texts for years when the Fire element energy is missing. 2012 is just such a year and homes whose Southeast sectors are thus protected will stay safe from this Five Yellow affliction.

Suppressing the Star 7 in the Northwest

The 7 star wreaked some real havoc last year, bringing violence, death and suffering to many countries in the Middle East, as well as into households whose central sector were somehow not protected against this afflictive number.

This year the number 7 flies to the Northwest, directly affecting the luck and prospects of the patriarch of households. This usually refers to the man of the family and to the leaders of countries and companies.

It brings danger of robbery and violence to those living in this part of the home; and in the office, if your desk is located here, chances are you could feel the negativity of being betrayed and let down.

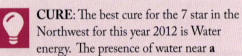

CURE: The best cure for the 7 star in the Northwest for this year 2012 is Water energy. The presence of water near **a Blue Elephant and a Blue Rhinoceros** would be extremely auspicious and this is because the metal element of the Northwest strengthens the 7 star. Water is needed to weaken the Metal energy.

Subduing the Star 3 in the Southwest

In 2012 the hostile quarrelsome star number 3 flies into the location of the matriarch i.e. the Southwest. This suggests that angry mood swings afflict the mother energy of homes affecting the harmony of families and the safety of marriages.

Those whose bedrooms are located in the Southwest will be especially influenced by this star number and they should make every effort to suppress it with strong fire energy. The number 3 star is a Wood element star and it is best dealt with using Fire energy.

This star number attracts the bad luck of having to cope with problems arising from the law. Court cases, litigation and quarrelsome energy will make life extremely difficult and aggravating for you if you are somehow affected by it. If your door faces the Southwest, it is best to try using another door and you should definitely try to increase lighting in this part of the house to suppress the 3 star.

CHAPTER 1 : DRAGON YEAR 2012

For the Horse born, if your bedroom is located in the Southwest, do be extra careful during the month of August as that is when someone could well find reason to fight with you or even take you to court. Note the remedies to overcome the number 3 star.

> **CURE FOR THE #3 STAR**:
> In 2012, the best cure for the number 3 star would be the **Magic Diagram Red Sword Mirror** which can suppress all hostile energy brought by other people's jealous intentions. This is a powerful feng shui implement that is very effective for slicing through the negative intentions of others aimed at you. Placed in the Southwest, this cure strengthens the chi essence of the Mother figure in households.

24 MOUNTAINS CHART OF 2012

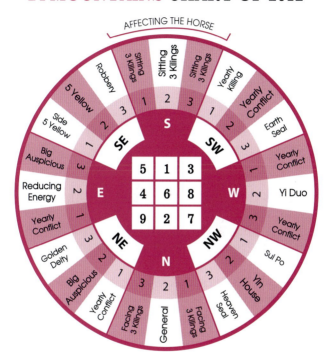

The Horse suffers from the Three Killings affliction brought by the 24 Mountains and hence should carry the the three celestial guardians as a cure. You however also enjoy the Victory Star this year, so you will be able to come out on top even in difficult situations.

THE STARS OF THE 24 MOUNTAINS

We also examine a third set of data which influence what the year brings to each of the twelve animal signs. These are the compass fortune stars of the 24 mountains, which change each year. Their influence on the luck profile of animal signs is meaningful, and working to subdue their negative influences or enhance their positive ones is an excellent way of improving one's fortunes for the year.

Different lucky and unlucky fortune stars fly into each of the 24 compass sectors each year, bringing energies that either improve or decrease the energy of the 12 animal signs.

There are 108 different fortune stars, but only a handful fly into each of the 24 mountain directions in any year. These bring auspicious or harmful influences, which vary in strength and type each year. The stars for 2012 are not as full of promise as they were last year.

This year we see a big number of conflict stars suggesting that the signs affected are in conflict with the year. Conflict signs are not auspicious; nor do they bring anything but disharmony and obstacles, so those affected should strive to either use amulet or gem therapy to counter the potential conflict brought by the compass fortune stars.

> Gem therapy uses the power of planetary influences and usually calls on activating one's favorable planets based on each animal sign's lucky days of birth - which can be their *Day of Excellence* or their *Day of Vitality*.

Animal signs that are negatively affected by the stars of the 24 Mountains should wear the "gemstone" that activates the planet that strengthens their day of vitality, and if possible, also their Day of Excellence.

So it is useful to know the gemstone to wear that will help you subdue 24 mountain star afflictions such as conflict stars, that are stationed at or near your Zodiac sign location.

Each day of the week is ruled by one of the seven powerful planets, which can be activated by wearing the gemstone associated with the planet.

⊙ **The SUN** enhances Sundays and the gemstone which strengthens the energy of the Sun are all the red colored stones - rubies, rubellites and red tourmalines.

CHAPTER 1 : DRAGON YEAR 2012

☾ **The MOON** strengthens the energy of Mondays and gemstones associated with the Moon are light colored pearls (preferably white) and the Moonstone. Crystals are also good for nurturing Moon energy to strengthen Mondays.

♂ **The planet MARS** nurtures the energy of Tuesdays and Mars is associated with red colored stones, although it is coral rather than any of the beryls or crystal stones that strengthens Mars.

☿ **The planet MERCURY** enhances Wednesdays and gemstones associated with this planet are all the green stones, which include jade, emeralds, as well as green tourmalines.

♃ **The planet JUPITER** enhances Thursdays and gemstones associated with this planet are all the yellow colored stones, the best of which are yellow diamonds and sapphires, although citrines are also excellent for pacifying Jupiter.

♀ **The planet VENUS** rules Friday and the gemstones associated with this planet are all the light blue colored stones such as aquamarines and blue topazes.

♄ **The planet SATURN** rules Saturdays and the gemstones associated with this planet are the dark blue sapphires.

In 2012, those of you born in the Year of the Horse are afflicted by the Star of 3 Killings. In fact the entire 90 degrees of the South are afflicted by this serious affliction which brings 3 kinds of losses - loss of wealth, loss of good name & loss of loved one.

Unfortunately for you, your element synchronizations with the year are average, so unless you strongly suppress these 3 Killings energies, you are not going to be very happy with the aggravations that the year sends to you.

For you, it is important to generate the aura of the **Three Celestial Guardians** - the Pi Yao, Chi Lin and Fu Dog. These can subdue the three killings energy. But you also need to enhance your Day of Vitality and Excellence, which are Friday (ruled by Venus) and Tuesday (ruled by Mars) respectively.

Wearing faceted light blue stones such as the aquamarines and matte red stones such as red coral can help the Horse subdue the aggravating chi energy brought by the three killings.

For the Horse, wearing light blue stones such as aquamarines, or red stones such as red coral, can subdue the afflictions brought this Dragon Year.

Meanwhile, also note that your **Day of Obstacles** is **Wednesday**, so you should **refrain from wearing green stones that activate the planet Mercury**, as doing so brings obstacles & aggravations into your life.

Watch out for the Three Killings

Remember that the "killing" stars are even more harmful than the conflict stars as killing energy always suggest the serious possibility of loss. In 2012 the stars of three killings bringing three kinds of loss afflict the three mountain sectors of the South. So even if you do not stay here, if you have doors located in the South you should also place the Guardians here.

 CURE FOR THE 3 KILLINGS: The most powerful remedy against killing energy are the **3 celestial creatures - the Chi Lin, Fu Dog and Pi Yao**. Images of these three creatures newly-made will have fresh and strong energy, and these should be placed in the South corners of the house and frequently used rooms that are located in the South to keep the three killings subdued. If your staircases and corridors are located in the South, it is a good idea to place the celestials there. Staircases and corridors are conduits of energy. Keeping negative energy out of such areas of the home keeps the household humming along harmoniously.

Beneficial Signs

Two directions benefit from the 24 mountains, and these are Southwest 3 and Northwest 3, both of which directions enjoy the good fortune of receiving the Earth and Heaven Seals respectively.

The good thing about these seals is that if only just one member or resident of a household enjoys the support of the heaven or earth seal, based on their animal sign - in this case the Monkey and the Boar respectively - it benefits the whole household.

> **ENHANCER**: It is definitely auspicious to activate the seals and this is easily done by having the Seal of Heaven in the Northwest 3 location and the Earth Seal in the Southwest 3 location. The **Heaven Seal** should be made in Metal and the **Earth Seal** should be made in crystal.

This year's 24 Mountains energy pattern manifests only two stars of *Big Auspicious* and these occur in the East 3 location and the Northeast 2 location. So those of you Horses whose bedrooms are located in these sectors of the home will benefit from these Big Auspicious stars.

Remember that when your personal energy is enhanced by good stars, good fortune gets multiplied and misfortune stars are subdued. However, not many people know that it is essential to be mentally and physically strong to benefit from good fortune stars.

Those whose mental attitudes are stable and strong always attract good fortune a lot more easily than those who give in easily to frustrations - getting weepy or angry too easily.

Some describe this as having intrinsic confidence, and so it is, but confidence comes from having the mental strength and chi essence to stay upbeat and optimistic. The Horse does not have a huge store of this in 2012, but you do have enough to build on. If you make an effort to enhance your own sense of self worth, your confidence will likewise gets strengthened.

A good store of yang vigor is always needed to actualize good fortune. It is your own confidence that provides the all-important missing factor, the third dimension to your luck - this is the cosmic empowerment of the self. It is this that makes the difference between having merely mediocre or enjoying truly outstanding luck. Success follows this kind of luck effortlessly.

Keeping Track of Your Good Months

Every year we emphasize the huge importance of timing in the way you manage your year and in how you can ensure that the important decisions you make as well as the actions you take through the course of the year are done at times when your luck is riding high.

As such, tracking the astrological flight of monthly stars is important, as this is what lets you see what months bring good energy and what months are better for you to avoid making important decisions or taking important action.

In these books we examine the way the monthly stars affect each of the 12 signs to include detailed analysis of your luck month by month. This gives you a blueprint for when to lie low and when to strike out, take risks and start projects dear to you. These monthly analyses highlight timely warnings that enable you to avoid accidents, avoid meeting up with bad people, getting burgled or succumbing to health risks. Good and bad months for travel are likewise highlighted.

Monthly updates analyze each month's Lo Shu numbers, element, trigram and paht chee luck pillars.

These pinpoint your lucky and unlucky months and give valuable pointers on how to navigate safely and successfully through the year.

Aggravating obstacles can be avoided; whatever misfortune vibes that lie ahead can be circumnavigated. You can then take timely precautions either by installing remedies or by making sure you wear the necessary protection to avoid these obstacles altogether.

The monthly updates are an important component of these books as recommendations are detailed and clear cut. Through the years we have received hundreds of thank you letters from readers telling us how they successfully followed our books and reduced the impact of accidents, burglaries and illnesses.

Improving Luck Using Compass Directions

In 2012, the use of correct facing and sitting directions - i.e. activating your personalized lucky directions - will help you stay protected against inadvertently getting hit by unlucky or disastrous transformational energies. So we have devoted a larger section this year on helping you to get your facing directions right. These are customized to assist all Horse-born to finetune their lucky and unlucky Kua directions.

CHAPTER 1 : DRAGON YEAR 2012

Compass Direction Feng Shui

This is one of the more effective ways of making sure the energies around you help rather than hinder you, no matter what you may be engaging in through the year. The energies of the 2012 Dragon Year are strong and particularly compelling, with good and bad luck making a big impact on people's lives.

The Dragon's powerful energy needs to be controlled and managed. It is a minefield of a year in terms of belligerence and violence, anger and antagonism; these hostile vibes are strongly prevalent. It is a year when the three celestials - Dragon, Tiger and Phoenix desperately need the calming effect of the celestial cosmic Tortoise.

The aura of the Tortoise is legendary and having its presence can be very beneficial. But getting your directions right while sleeping, working, eating, talking and so forth will also go a long way towards safeguarding your luck this year. Do take this advice seriously. It is really no fun being hit by bad energy; this will happen if you inadvertently face a direction that is out of sync with your sign especially when doing something important or when talking to someone important. The key is to activate directions that are lucky for you and lucky this year as well.

Spiritual Feng Shui

Finally, as something new, we are including in this year's books a whole section on Spiritual Feng Shui which includes a special section on the power of amulets, focusing in especially on the amulet best suited to your sign of the Horse.

There are amulets and rituals that ward off bad luck, protect against being obstructed in your business and your career, as well as to attract specific kinds of good fortune for those building a new house, having a baby, starting a new venture, getting married, embarking on a long journey or needing cosmic assistance on a specific project.

Amulets may be worn on special chakra points of the body or displayed in certain corners of frequently used rooms. This is part of the Third Dimension of feng shui, a dimension that makes the practice of feng shui much more complete. Different animal signs benefit from different kinds of amulets, and wearing those that are best for your sign will help you to stay on top of the elements affecting you during the year.
In astrology, keeping the elements balanced is the key to unlocking good fortune, but when this is helped along by cosmic Sanskrit symbols and powerful mantras, the effect becomes incredibly potent as it

taps directly into the cosmic power of spiritual feng shui. By bringing in the third dimension, we will also be enhancing the feng shui of our living spaces. Space is enhanced with environmental feng shui methods through the optimum placement of furniture and auspicious objects.

Good space feng shui also means good design of layout and flow of chi. It takes note of compass directions on a personalized basis and uses other methods to identify lucky and unlucky sectors. Broadly speaking, it takes care of the Earth aspect in the trinity of luck.

Time dimension feng shui addresses energy pattern changes over time and is founded on the premise that energy is never static but constantly changing. This means good feng shui requires regular updating by taking into account overlapping cycles of time; annually, monthly, daily, hourly and even in larger time frames that last 20 years and 60 years. It takes 180 years to complete a full 9 period cycle of 20 years. These books address the annual and monthly cycles of change that affect everyone differently. These cycles are viewed within the larger context of the Period of 8 cycle, which deals with the heavenly cosmic forces within the trinity of luck.

> Using, wearing and displaying amulets is part of the spiritual third dimension, which focuses on energies generated by mankind. In concert with cosmic forces, the strength of amulets is derived from the individual's own yang chi, and this is created by the mind's connections to the cosmos.

Self energy in its purest form is the most powerful kind of energy. This is Mankind Chi which combines with heaven and earth to create the trinity of luck. The empowered self generates copious amounts of positive spiritual chi and this can be directed into amulets to empower them.

When consecrated (i.e. energized) by Masters who possess highly concentrated energies through their superior practices, these amulets take on great potency. To possess concentrated spiritual power requires years of practice; there are methods - both gross and subtle - that can be learnt which are collectively part of the inner feng shui traditions of feng shui.

In the old days, Masters of the old school were great adepts at these kinds of transcendental practice and they often made special amulets with their knowledge, to give to those who came to them for help. Some of these amulets were made according to the animal sign of birth of those asking for them.

These Masters were devotees of Taoist or Buddhist spiritual deities; many increased their own cosmic powers through regular daily meditations, reciting powerful mantras and sutras and using secret rituals to remove obstacles.

In the practice of astrological traditions, the Tibetan practitioners of cosmic magic generally invoke powerful Buddhist deities who awaken within these individuals their own inner forces, sometimes bringing them to pretty high levels of siddhic accomplishments. This aspect of feng shui or luck invocation has only rarely been leaked out into the world. Many of the most effective methods and rituals, sutras and magical mantras are still secret, or have not yet been translated. Masters familiar with these practices reveal their secrets only to a favored few.

A few of these secrets have made their way to us, and one discovery we have made are the secrets related to creating and consecrating amulets according to the animal sign of birth. For the Horse, we have included here an amulet which will benefit you just by carrying this book near you. We have also discovered that powerful incense rituals using specially formulated aromas and offered to the local cosmic protectors can be used to overcome life and success obstacles.

For the Horse-born, we recommend that you use incense to clear all bad luck during the months of **April**, **June**, **August** & **September** this year, and also to dispel burglary luck in January of 2013. Doing so will help subdue the different kinds of troubled afflictions that come during these months.

Incense rituals can remove obstacles and make your path to success smoother and a lot less aggravating.

CHAPTER 1 : DRAGON YEAR 2012

Amulet for the Horse-born. Carrying this amulet near you at all times will keep you safe from harmful energies through the year.

Chapter Two
THE HORSE IN 2012
Luck Prospects & Energy Strength

- Water Horse – 70 years
- Wood Horse – 58 years
- Fire Horse – 46 years
- Earth Horse – 34 years
- Metal Horse – 22 years
- Water Horse – 10 years

Outlook for the Horse In 2012

All the elements that signify the five types of luck change in 2012, reflecting the transformational nature of the year's energy. For the Horse, the new year brings substantial reduction in its inner chi strength and life force, and this is something that will be strongly felt by the Horse through the Year of the Dragon.

The level of both your life force and your chi essence this year dips significantly from last year, indicating a lessening in the overall luck you will enjoy this year. It is however not a year when you need to pull back and rein in because you are blessed this year with some friendly feng shui winds which help you steady yourself and stay standing. In other words, you are weaker this year, but not necessarily defeated. On the contrary, the victory star of 1 rekindles your sporting spirit.

What this means is that in 2012 you will need to work harder, run faster & stay ever vigilant for the main chance.

Success luck is not stable. There will be fluctuations through the year, but you will benefit from your own intrinsic strengths. These enable you to outrun others in the same game, and on occasions, you can emerge victorious. You will do especially well in competitive situations, especially those where you participate on your own.

But you also need to understand that victory does not come easy, or with any substantial tangible gains. The rewards of your pursuits do not bring much by way of winnings either in cash or in kind. Nevertheless, coming ahead of others will give you a psychic high.

This successfully makes your spirits soar, bringing a joyousness to the year for you. Nevertheless, the year will leave you feeling philosophical, which is a good thing. This year the Horse that enjoys the most success luck is the Water Horse, but you are either a **10 year old** or a **70 year old**, so for you, success has rather less real meaning than for your other Horse colleagues.

The other Horses unfortunately will meet up with obstacles that hinder their progress and growth in 2012. In fact, it seems wise to lower your expectations for the year. When you do not expect much, even the little you gain will be sweet.

This is also not a good year to start anything too risky or difficult. Better to keep doing work you are familiar with than go out on a limb hoping to break new ground. The outlook for your financial stability is also not terribly promising.

Except for **46 year old Fire Horse**, the rest of you could even lose a small amount of money and experience some close calls. If you are smart, you would take a cool attitude towards risky investments. Better to stay conservative rather than test your hard-earned assets against unknowns. This is not a good year to take those kinds of chances.

Beware the Three Killings

The Horse must take note that the stars of the 24 Mountains are also not helpful to your luck. What you will be up against this year are the three killings stars - and these are not easy to subdue given your low levels of life force and chi essence.

These harmful and afflictive stars play havoc with your moods and mental stability, and you definitely need the protection of the three celestial creatures - the Chi Lin, Fu Dog and Pi Yao - who collectively can help you ward off the worst of the three killings afflictions.

Resist any urge to gallop off into the fray trying to win by sheer force of determination and speed, qualities you are known for. In 2012, the cosmic energies of the year are not in your favor, so it is advisable to go easy on yourself.

Be more of a watcher than a participant, and should you want to do anything special or take a risk, choose your timing carefully. The good news for the Horse is that this is a year when there are many months when the localized energy works in your favor. This may not be as strong as your annual element energies, but they are usually strong enough for you to come out on top in your day-to-day exploits.

For all Horses, this year appears favorable mainly to indulge your love of fast sports as there is no real danger to your life force, and when the stakes are not too high. In other words, enjoy the year. Just do not take financial risks. Success is something that will prove elusive this year but this does not mean you cannot enjoy your year. Just engage in activities that do not have a high emotional or economic price tag and you will do well this year.

The luck of the five kinds of Horse based on the element interactions of their heavenly stems with those of year are indicated as follows. This reflects the Horse's overall luck for the year:

Water Horse – Superb health luck

Wood Horse – Soften your stance to win.

Fire Horse – Financial luck shines brightly

Earth Horse – Perseverance brings recognition

Metal Horse – Moving forward steadily

CHAPTER 2 : LUCK OF THE HORSE IN 2012

OUTLOOK FOR THE HORSE IN 2012

The Horse is better off being carefree and relaxed. No need for painstaking analysis of life situations; in matters of love relationships, it is better to simplify your life and embrace whatever is your situation this year or keep an open mind to whatever happens. This will be a time when you will not easily get excited over new friends. In fact, nothing appears too exciting. This is a year when you create your own excitement and in many ways, you also create your own luck.

The main thing about the Horse personality is that you are a creature blessed with natural grace and great fortitude. There is an independence of thought which makes you a strong individual, able to assess situations, good at pacing yourself and knowing when to lie low and when to gallop ahead.

The Horse may be a free spirit, but this is not an irresponsible person. You have the confidence of knowing what your shortcomings are in any given situation so that in 2012, you will do your best to blend seamlessly into the transformational energy of the year. The Dragon Year can be loud and boisterous and the Horse may well feel out of it. But irrespective of how the year's energies sync with yours, you should have no difficulty blending in, keeping your thoughts to yourself and playing your cards close to your chest. Be as aggressive as you wish in trying to win, professionally and commercially, or for the sheer fun of it. But do not play dirty or try underhand tactics as this is simply not you. The Horse is a creature of high principles to whom integrity is an important attribute.

So irrespective of where you work or what you do, whether you are a business person or working for someone or for some company, play fair this year and stay true to yourself despite the temptation to cut corners here and there... even just a little can quickly become a habit.

From time to time, you could be overcome by tough situations, and that is when you need to check yourself. Here is where being blessed by the number 1 star is so auspicious, because the number 1 star is a white star that shines with brilliance and steadfastness in the midst of any kind of difficult situation.

With this kind of feng shui energy, the Horse is unlikely to lose too much sleep over what might have been.

CHAPTER 2 : LUCK OF THE HORSE IN 2012

Never looking backwards, always looking forwards, the Horse is sharply aware of the greater cosmic energies that bring a scenario of change to the year.

There are also major afflictive stars in 2012 that cause even the best laid plans to go awry, so if anything happens during the year that forces you to change direction, it benefits you to make the best of the situation. In 2012 go with the energy flow of the world. Accept that is a year of powerful transformational developments and you can sail through effortlessly. What is most disturbing however is of an astrological nature. In 2012, the Horse is surrounded by the seriously afflicted energies of the three killings. So there is a need for the correct cure here to suppress the bad vibes created.

> **CURE FOR THE THREE KILLINGS**: You can display the three celestial guardians together in your South direction to help you overcome the most current stars of three killings. These three are **the Chi Lin, Fu Dog and Pi Yao** and you can place all three on the entire South section of your home or your room. This subdues the three killings very effectively, helping you to avoid the afflictions that are directly in your sector.

It is unfortunate that there does not appear to be any auspicious stars lurking nearby, so this will be a year when you need to depend very much on yourself, on what you can create and how you make something admirable and auspicious out of very little help from the "stars".

This is not as difficult as it sounds because the element of "mankind luck" can often attract even bigger and better things into one's life than simply depending on the "heavens" to help you. Think through what you want from the year and give it your empowerment!

> **FENG SHUI ENHANCER**:
> To generate good mankind luck, consider placing something very red and very yang in the South corner as this will create Fire energy to strengthen the element of this sector. Display the **red crystal ball with the heart sutra** or place the **Hum lampshade** here in your home location. The all-powerful Hum syllable, kept activated by the light of the lampshade is very auspicious and protective.

Keep the lampshade turned on daily, and if you can, add crystal globes under the lampshade as this will bring great harmony into your life and your home. Crystal balls have enormous capacity to absorb conflict vibes especially when there is a light activating them. This should take care of the yearly conflict star on the left of your home location in the compass wheel this year.

> Do make an effort to keep the lights in your South location a little brighter than usual as this adds to the store of Fire element energy. Note that Fire is missing in the year's chart, so Fire is always welcome in 2012.

The Horse is definitely going to have a very unstable time in its many relationships. Professionally and in your personal life, you will find that there seem to be hidden tensions causing you some perplexity. Those who are married might want to consider having a "happiness occasion" in the form of a new baby or a marriage of one of your children.

Should there indeed be such a "*hei*" occasion in your household, welcome it as a very good sign. Having a yang-type function will activate the Dragon Year and act as a magnet for good fortune vibes to come your way. You can also create such an occasion by throwing a yang evening of festivities celebrating the birthday of an older person in the family.

CHAPTER 2 : LUCK OF THE HORSE IN 2012

In your interactions with others however, this is not a particularly easy year. You might seem unreasonable to others, but that simply reflects the influences of the 2012 stars. No need to try making excuses for yourself or to complain and explain; the best way to even out the blips in your relationships is to shrug your shoulders and smile your way through the high tension moments.

Horses, especially those who are young and just starting out in working life, tend to be impulsive and quick to judgement. It is possible your volatile streak will reveal itself although what does it matter? In this Year of the Dragon, you can be as obvious as you wish showcasing your ambitions; but this can grate on the nerves of others and will not win you friends at work.

Perhaps subduing your exuberance is a good idea, or try pairing up with your ally, the Tiger, as this is excellent feng shui for you, causing you to be less obvious and direct, and more diplomatic. The Tiger is your ally so there is a natural fit here. Also note that your respective Lo Shu numbers this year are 1 and 9 making a sum-of-ten combination. Getting a Tiger ally really does make a big difference to your luck this year.

OUTLOOK FOR THE LADY HORSE IN 2012

The Lady Horse is spirited, saucy and stunningly independent, perhaps every adventurous man's secret dream girl. She is the ultimate sport, game for whatever is suggested and very agreeable within any social group. Irrespective of her social background, she is usually down-to-earth, not at all grand and incredibly good at making friends and reaching out to others. Whether she comes from a rich family background or from more modest beginnings, the Horse lady is proud of who she is and what she is at any moment in time.

BIRTH YEAR	TYPE OF HORSE LADY	LO SHU NO.	AGE	LUCK OUTLOOK IN 2012
1942	Water Horse Lady	4	70	A very good year to relax and invest
1954	Wood Horse Lady	1	58	Do not take risks this year
1966	Fire Horse Lady	7	46	Financial luck is stable, but go slow
1978	Earth Horse Lady	4	34	Strength of purpose motivates you
1990	Metal Horse Lady	1	22	Not a year to be too adventurous
2002	Water Horse Girl	7	10	Good recognition & results

The Year of the Dragon however brings some de-stabilizing influence to her usual exuberance, causing rather extreme mood swings that affect her relationship with those she works with. It can also be a rather more stressful year than the previous year and she feels exhausted more easily.

The Lady Horse could find the year's cosmic energies draining, so she is not at her best this year. Her special vitality is less forthcoming, so it really is essential that she does not overtax herself or strain her resources. It is advisable to take life a little slower; so a change of pace is beneficial.

Her personal Life Force does not look at all encouraging and there will be moments when her energy gives out. Her attitudes too will yo-yo, although this does improve and gets increasingly stable as the year wears on, peaking in December.

Underneath that veneer of good natured kindliness and happy-go-lucky boisterousness beats a heart of gold… and a mind that is as agile as her personality. The Horse lady can be super efficient and can get things done in half the time it takes others. Despite this, her friends and colleagues should not expect too much of her this year as she is really not operating at full capacity in 2012. There is much that is untapped in this sign. This is a year best spent pursuing an ordinary kind of lifestyle with few big moments.

The Dragon Year this time around is transformational, and the energies can be conflicting. They are not conducive to going out on a limb and taking unnecessary risks. So the lady Horse is better off staying housebound rather than doing too much travelling.

> The Lady Horse is at heart a free spirit. She values her personal freedom enormously but she also has a very clear sense of her own identity.

To her, being courageous is as important as being successful, so when confronted with choices, she will not impulsively go only for the option that brings greater glory and recognition. If she has to disagree, she will do so even at the risk of sacrificing her own personal success.

It is not possible to completely tame or subdue the lady horse, not even in a year like 2012 when she could well throw up her hands at the trials and obstacles blocking her way. In spite of Life Force and Chi Strength being at an average level only, she will always be conscious of being her own person. The Horse rarely loses her sense of self, even though when taken to extremes, this need to feel free can consume those around her.

In 2012, **the 34 year old Earth Horse** throws work concerns to the winds to do 'her thing". This works for her, but if the **22 year old Metal Hors**e does anything too way out, it could bring danger. Actually, this is a year when you are better off being surrounded by things and people familiar to you. Going into a whole new environment can throw open a whole slew of problems.

CHAPTER 2 : LUCK OF THE HORSE IN 2012

OUTLOOK FOR THE GENTLEMAN HORSE IN 2012

The Gentleman Horse enters the Dragon Year feeling constrained and a little unsettled. This is a very free spirited human being not prone to moods, but the energies of the year make him less confident than usual. So we see a Horse guy who is indecisive and uncertain, yet who will make every effort not to show his vulnerability.

Despite this and the various cosmic obstacles he will face this year, the Horse guy is no less assertive.

BIRTH YEAR	TYPE OF HORSE MAN	LO SHU NO.	AGE	LUCK OUTLOOK IN 2012
1942	Water Horse Man	4	70	Things move very smoothly for you
1954	Wood Horse Man	1	58	Obstacles cause you aggravation
1966	Fire Horse Man	7	46	Monetary gains but little growth
1978	Earth Horse Man	4	34	Your determination fuels you
1990	Metal Horse Man	1	22	Better to lie low, keep your head down
2002	Water Horse Boy	7	10	Good recognition & results

He will be as demanding and even, in some cases, as active as ever. It takes a lot to get the Horse to slow down, but in 2012, this is something he will do of his own accord. The cosmic energy around him will force him to take intermittent breaks, not just to rest, but also to take stock of the situation facing him through the year.

The gentleman Horse will be a less dominating individual in 2012, and also slightly more inhibited than usual. This is evident during the summer months when feng shui winds bring more problems than ever.

The reality of the year will tend to have a humbling effect on the Horse personality, so many people could find you a great deal more subdued and also less showy.

This is not a bad thing as you do buckle down to work, although for many of you, attaining your desires can be difficult. Luck is not much on your side when it comes to getting what you want. But your confidence grows as the year progresses and your luck peaks in December. That is when your usual self becomes more evident.

The essential attributes of the Horse sign tend to be very macho and masculine, and their "horsey" traits tend to be exaggerated in the gentleman Horse. They tend to be regarded as being more passionate and seductive than their female counterparts. But they can be very obstinate, more so than the females of their sign.

Horses need **sunlight** and **yang chi** to bring out the best in them, more so the gentleman of the sign. So they tend to be more active and robust during the summer months. This is the season when their energy levels are at a high and in fact, it is widely believed that Horses born in the summer almost always do better in life than those born in the dreary months of Fall or Winter, just as Horses born in the daylight yang hours are usually more energetic than those born in the night.

ENERGY STRENGTH ANALYSIS OF HORSE LUCK 2012

This section focuses on the element luck analyses of the Horse in 2012. These reveal five kinds of luck in the Horse horoscope and are charted according to how the Horse's ruling luck elements in the year of birth interacts with the elements of the year 2012, thus offering indications of strength or weakness in the horoscope for the year.

Check the tables in the following pages to take note of your five luck categories in 2012. The significance of the luck indications is explained as follows:

First, Your Life Force…

This highlights the hidden dangers to your life. Danger to one's life manifests suddenly and with little warning. In the past two years, clashing elements in the paht chee chart brought raging wildfires, tsunamis, floods, earthquakes and other natural disasters that wreaked havoc and destruction. Last year, this was compounded by the feng shui chart which brought the violent star 7 to the centre, so we saw raw human anger overflow into revolution that brought danger into the lives of millions of people. Many of these uprisings and disasters happened without warning. Staying safe against being caught unawares is an important aspect of horoscope readings.

Those born in Horse years have a very average level of Life Force luck, registering at OX for 2012. This means that your life force is neither strong nor weak, indicating that the year should be reasonably safe for you, although it is a good idea to be alert to signs of danger.

There is no big need to worry despite turbulence of the world's energies and the instability of natural forces. But wearing protective amulets is worthwhile doing just to keep and stay safe.

Second, Your Health Luck...

This is the luck of your health condition during the year and it indicates how strongly you can avoid illness bugs. For the Horse, note that the feng shui chart brings good strong winds that suggest your health is not weak. But **22 year old Metal Horse** should be careful as you have a **XX** against your health window. When the luck indication is a double **XX**, it means that 2012 can bring ailments which cause obstacles to success. Plans get blocked. Opportunities thus get missed easily.

Third, Your Finance Luck...

This reveals if you will enjoy financial stability during the year. It is also an indication of whether you can do better than the previous year.

The highest showing of wealth luck is a double **OO** and this is for the **46 year old Fire Horse**. This means that financial luck is stable and there could be some extra income coming your way in 2012.

CHAPTER 2 : LUCK OF THE HORSE IN 2012

The 58 year old Wood Horse and the 22 year old Metal Horse could suffer through a year of unstable money luck. For you two, better to introduce some wealth rituals into your day to day living to overcome this. Note that both these Horse signs are showing X against their Finance Luck, with the Metal Horse indicating a single X & the Wood Horse a double XX.

An indication of crosses is a negative reading and the more crosses there are the greater the instability of your financial situation. One of the best ways of enhancing wealth luck is to invoke the presence of the Wealth Buddhas; by wearing the moving mantra watch featuring **Yellow Dzambhala holding a Rat spewing forth jewels** or **White Dzambhala sitting on a Dragon**.

If your Finance Luck is down, as indicated this year for the 58 year old Wood Horse and the 22 year old Metal Horse, it is a good idea to wear the White Dzambala moving mantra watch to enhance wealth and prosperity luck.

97

Fourth, Your Success Luck...

This highlights your attainment luck for the year whether it be success in your professional work or in your studies. Circles are strong indications of success while **XX**s are negative indications suggesting obstacles.

The luck indication for all of you born in Horse years is that you have to live through a double **XX** indication. This means there are obstacles to your success luck this year. Promotions could be hard to come by, although not impossible. But an **XX** against the success luck category is not a very encouraging sign.

Fifth, Your Spirit Essence...

This indicator of Chi Essence luck reveals insights into your inner resilience and spiritual strength. When strong, it shows you are resistant to spiritual afflictions and can more easily overcome the lack of other categories of luck. Low Spirit Essence is indicated by crosses, and this instantly tells you to be careful and to protect yourself with powerful mantra amulets. The Horse has an **OX** reading against its chi essence luck and this means that your inner spirit is only of average strength.

CHAPTER 2 : LUCK OF THE HORSE IN 2012

To enhance your chi essence you should wear protective mantras touching you and on your body. These can be worn as rings or as pendants; best with powerful seed syllables *Hum* or *Bhrum*, both of which are excellent to lift your spirits.

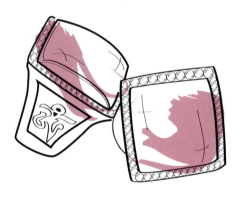

To counter low Spirit Essence, wear the seed syllable *Hum* or *Bhrum* as a pendant or ring. This provides protection against spirit harm.

CHAPTER 2 : LUCK OF THE HORSE IN 2012

WATER HORSE
70 YEARS OLD

TYPE OF LUCK	ELEMENT AT BIRTH	ELEMENT IN 2012	LUCK RATING
LIFE FORCE	FIRE	EARTH	OX
HEALTH LUCK	WOOD	WATER	OOO
FINANCE LUCK	WATER	WATER	O
SUCCESS LUCK	METAL	WOOD	OO
SPIRIT ESSENCE	WOOD	FIRE	OX

WOOD HORSE
58 YEARS OLD

TYPE OF LUCK	ELEMENT AT BIRTH	ELEMENT IN 2012	LUCK RATING
LIFE FORCE	FIRE	WOOD	OX
HEALTH LUCK	METAL	WOOD	OO
FINANCE LUCK	WOOD	METAL	XX
SUCCESS LUCK	METAL	FIRE	XX
SPIRIT ESSENCE	WOOD	WATER	OX

CHAPTER 2 : **LUCK OF THE HORSE IN 2012**

FIRE HORSE
46 YEARS OLD

TYPE OF LUCK	ELEMENT AT BIRTH	ELEMENT IN 2012	LUCK RATING
LIFE FORCE	FIRE	WOOD	OX
HEALTH LUCK	WATER	WOOD	OX
FINANCE LUCK	FIRE	METAL	OO
SUCCESS LUCK	METAL	FIRE	XX
SPIRIT ESSENCE	WOOD	WATER	OX

EARTH HORSE
34 YEARS OLD

TYPE OF LUCK	ELEMENT AT BIRTH	ELEMENT IN 2012	LUCK RATING
LIFE FORCE	FIRE	WOOD	OX
HEALTH LUCK	FIRE	WOOD	OOO
FINANCE LUCK	EARTH	METAL	OX
SUCCESS LUCK	METAL	FIRE	XX
SPIRIT ESSENCE	WOOD	WATER	OX

CHAPTER 2 : LUCK OF THE HORSE IN 2012

METAL HORSE
22 YEARS OLD

TYPE OF LUCK	ELEMENT AT BIRTH	ELEMENT IN 2012	LUCK RATING
LIFE FORCE	FIRE	WOOD	OX
HEALTH LUCK	EARTH	WOOD	OOO
FINANCE LUCK	METAL	METAL	X
SUCCESS LUCK	METAL	FIRE	XX
SPIRIT ESSENCE	WOOD	WATER	OX

WATER HORSE
10 YEARS OLD

TYPE OF LUCK	ELEMENT AT BIRTH	ELEMENT IN 2012	LUCK RATING
LIFE FORCE	FIRE	EARTH	OX
HEALTH LUCK	METAL	WATER	OX
FINANCE LUCK	METAL	WATER	OX
SUCCESS LUCK	WATER	WOOD	OX
SPIRIT ESSENCE	WOOD	FIRE	OX

Chapter Three

PERSONALIZING YOUR FENG SHUI LUCK IN 2012

Individualized Directions to Protect Your Good Feng Shui

In 2012, the Horse sign benefits from the presence of the wish-fulfilling sky which brings victory and triumphant moments through the year for this sign. The power of ONE can be spectacular when your personal feng shui is also at its best, and in 2012, the Horse's Fire element helps to ensure there is a good balance of elements around its location. Fire is the missing element in the year's paht chee chart, so a sign like the Horse which is yang Fire benefits not only itself but also those around its sphere of influence.

CHAPTER 3 : PERSONALISING YOUR FENG SHUI LUCK

> **The number 1 is a Water element number and when placed in the South location of the Horse, which is Fire, there is friction and conflict energy generated UNLESS once again there is good feng shui energy created to enable Fire and Water to transform into powerful steam.**

This is done by introducing Wood element energy here. Water feeds the Wood which then feeds the Fire creating then a harmonious flow of the three elements. So do place plenty of plants in your South sector in 2012 to enhance the sector's feng shui to benefit the Horse.

It is however also important to know the energy of the Dragon Year is not as favorable for the Horse as in the previous year, but you have come out of the previous year of the Rabbit stronger and much revitalised. So even though your Life Force decreases a little this year, the Horse has the strength to cope with whatever obstacles may come its way due to the three killings energy around it.

This is a serious affliction although of course it can be handled and subdued using the powerful symbols

CHAPTER 3 : **PERSONALISING YOUR FENG SHUI LUCK**

of the celestial protectors - the Chi Lin, the Fu Dog and the Pi Yao. The presence of these creatures in your direction of South is usually sufficient to neutralize the effect of the three killings.

So the year can become a promising year for the Horse to continue building on what was achieved in the previous year. But you need to work on building your own self confidence, so that yours becomes a mindset of success. There is every reason for you to prosper and move upwards in this Year of the Dragon. The year will have its ups and downs, but on balance, you will start and end the year very well indeed and also feeling strong.

In terms of feng shui luck, what the Horse should do immediately is to give the home a thorough spring cleaning making sure the energy in all your living and work spaces are not left to stagnate.

This is equivalent of the five minutes of body shaking each morning, something which experts on energy highly recommend to ensure the chi within our bodies are kept moving each day when we wake up.

Shift your furniture to move your space chi. This allows air to flow through the hidden spaces of nooks

105

and corners and when you are done, move your furniture back. Use this exercise to clean hard to reach spaces. This is a powerful re-energising ritual which encourages energy to move, thus creating yang chi and bringing vibrant new energy into the home.

This should get you ready for the new year. This shaking and moving ritual also makes sure your life does not stagnate and that you will continue to grow steadily... and with vigor. It may sound simple, but this simple ritual is both effective and powerful.

Next you can customize the feng shui of your space first by activating the astrological location of your animal sign and second by using compass directions feng shui to maximise your luck for the year.

MAKING HORSE'S SOUTH 2 LOCATION AUSPICIOUS

The location of the Horse is South 2. You must know exactly where this part of your home is. This is your Horse location which you must pay special attention to. You must never for whatever reason at all leave this corner dirty, cluttered or worse, filled with rotting materials.

CHAPTER 3 : **PERSONALISING YOUR FENG SHUI LUCK**

This part of the home must reflect your care and attention and it should definitely not be your store room, nor your toilet and also try not to do any cooking in this part of the house or room.

It is vital to bring correct feng shui inputs to this part of the home, as well as to this South corner of all the rooms frequently used by you. The element of this space is Fire, while the incoming feng shui wind here in 2012 is Water, so this is superficially at least a conflict of element energies.

But as indicated, Fire and Water can be transformed into steam to bring enormous power to the surrounding cosmic realms. What is needed is presence of Wood i.e. healthy, well growing plants. If you can engineer a transformation of the Fire/Water conflict what is created is very auspicious.

The Water element energy flown into the South 2 sector does not hurt the Horse even though its element is Fire... if you introduce Wood element into the space. Then the sector's energy becomes supportive and powerful.

It is definitely beneficial for the Horse person to enhance the Wood element in the South sectors of the

CHAPTER 3 : PERSONALISING YOUR FENG SHUI LUCK

different rooms of your home. Here Wood feeds the Fire while exhausting the incoming Water brought by the number 1 thereby creating good balance and harmony of elements. So do bring plants into this part of your house to ensure good feng shui this year.

Place healthy plants in the South this year to introduce much needed Wood energy here. This will reconcile the Fire/Water clash, making the South (Horse's personal sector) very lucky indeed.

 ENHANCER FOR THE SOUTH: Place Wood-made symbols of the three celestial protectors here - the **Pi Yao, Fu Dog and Chi Lin**. Look for well made carvings of these creatures made of good hardwood or rosewood. They are not easy to find as it is not easy to make good well-defined carvings from hard wood, but whatever can be found usually has great strength, because hard wood is so dense and heavy.

It is for this reason the Chinese like the black woods so much because they are hard and very dense - so auspicious. These feng shui protectors will not only bring protective energy to the South sector but also enhance the Wood element here, hence transforming the Water with Fire combination of elements here.

ENHANCING YOUR PERSONAL LO SHU NUMBER

BIRTH YEAR	ELEMENT HORSE	AGE	LO SHU NUMBER AT BIRTH
1942	METAL HORSE	70	4
1954	WATER HORSE	58	1
1966	WOOD HORSE	46	7
1978	FIRE HORSE	34	4
1990	EARTH HORSE	22	1
2002	METAL HORSE	10	7

The Lo Shu number of Horse-born are 4, 1 or 7. The personalised Lo Shu interacts with the Lo Shu number of the year and your good luck during the year is either enhanced or afflicted by the way the numbers interact. The Lo Shu number of 2012 is the white number 6.

Horse with Birth Lo Shu of 4
(affecting the 70 & 34 year old Horse)

The number 4 creates a *Sum-of-Ten* combination with the number 6 bringing very auspicious completion luck to this 70 and 34 year old Horse.

This combination brings good relationship and wealth luck to you this year; they can sometimes also be read as an indication of marriage if it affects someone of marriageable age or who are eligible or looking for a mate. This combination also brings scholastic or academic recognition.

The feng shui enhancement for these Horse people and especially for those who are of the male gender is to enhance the East corner of the house with Water. The East is where the number 4 flies to in 2012 and there is thus a sum of ten here created with the Lo Shu number of the year. Installing a new **water feature** here brings wealth accumulation luck.

Horse with Birth Lo Shu of 1
(affecting the 58 & 22 year old Horse)

The number 1 creates a *Ho Tu* combination with the year's number of 6. This is a very auspicious indication which brings various forms of good fortune manifestation to the 58 year old and 22 year old Horse. This combination makes the year come alive with promise to these two Horse people, meaning success can be achieved.

What is started will be easily brought to a successful and auspicious conclusion. The combination of numbers indicate that enhancing the North with Water will greatly improve the luck of these two Horse people.

Horse with Birth Lo Shu of 7
(affecting the 46 & 10 year old Horse)

The Lo Shu number of this Horse has a neutral combination with the year's number 6. But the year's Lo Shu does bring unexpected support from people who may not know you very well. Note however that those of you who are in a leadership position will benefit in 2012, as the number 7 has flown in to the sector of the patriarch.

CHAPTER 3 : **PERSONALISING YOUR FENG SHUI LUCK**

> **ENHANCER**: Place a powerful figure of the **Kuan Kung, the Chinese God of Wealth and Victory** in the Northwest sector to activate your own Lo Shu of 7 this year. Get a figurine made of Metal - best is brass - and choose one whose face looks fierce. This benefits the male members of your family...

FINETUNING HORSE'S LUCKY DIRECTIONS IN 2012

The Eight Mansions formula of feng shui divides people into East and West groups, with each group having their own lucky and unlucky directions. To use Eight Mansions you need to first determine your auspicious directions and then you should make it a point to always face at least one of your good directions while working, negotiating, sleeping, eating or dating.

There are different lucky directions for MEN and for WOMEN and these are calculated using their lunar year of birth. Just doing this faithfully, using a good compass to determine the directions, will bring you instant good feng shui. This is also one of the easiest formulas of feng shui to use and the one which you are least likely to make a mistake with. Study your

CHAPTER 3 : PERSONALISING YOUR FENG SHUI LUCK

good and bad luck directions from the charts here. Note that the directions are different for each of the Kua numbers and also note that the Kua numbers are different for male and females.

AUSPICIOUS DIRECTIONS FOR HORSE FEMALES

BIRTH YEAR	AGE	ELEMENT/ KUA	HEALTH DIRECTION	SUCCESS DIRECTION	LOVE & FAMILY DIRECTION	PERSONAL GROWTH DIRECTION
1942	70	WATER/2	W	NE	NW	SW
1954	58	WOOD/5	NW	SW	W	NE
1966	46	FIRE/8	NW	SW	W	NE
1978	34	EARTH/2	W	NE	NW	SW
1990	22	METAL/5	NW	SW	W	NE
2002	10	WATER/8	NW	SW	W	NE

All Horse women belong to the West group of lucky directions and many of you are going through an auspicious time in the current Period of 8. You benefit from living in Southwest or Northeast facing houses, especially houses facing Southwest 1. All recently built Southwest or Northeast facing houses bring extreme good fortune to the Lady Horse.

CHAPTER 3 : **PERSONALISING YOUR FENG SHUI LUCK**

Indeed, the Success direction for all Horse women is either Southwest or Northeast. From now until Feb 4th 2024, houses facing Southwest or Northeast bring brilliant good fortune for their residents.

In terms of facing and living directions, they should sit, work, stand and sleep facing the Southwest, Northeast, West or Northwest but these basic good fortune directions must always be adjusted for the changing energies of each year, and thus in 2012, you need to see which of the directions that are good for you are "safe" to face. Thus do take note as follows:

- ▶ Do NOT face **Southwest** this year as this direction is afflicted by the presence of the hostile star. Facing Southwest may bring you luck but it is success that comes with a great deal of hostile energy.
- ▶ **Northeast** is lucky as it has the powerful star of 9 which brings future prosperity. So facing Northeast is auspicious.
- ▶ **West** is by far the strongest and luckiest of the West group directions in 2012, so do face this direction if you are a West group person.

CHAPTER 3 : PERSONALISING YOUR FENG SHUI LUCK

▶ The **Northwest** is afflicted with burglary energy so it is not a good direction to face in 2012. Normally the Northwest is excellent for patriarchs i.e. leaders, but the danger here this year is that the 7 star can play havoc with all your relationships. Better to stay safe and not face the Northwest direction this year.

AUSPICIOUS DIRECTIONS FOR HORSE MEN

Not all Horse men enjoy the same superior luck which their female counterparts enjoy in the current Period, but those belonging to the West group

BIRTH YEAR	AGE	ELEMENT/ KUA	HEALTH DIRECTION	SUCCESS DIRECTION	LOVE & FAMILY DIRECTION	PERSONAL GROWTH DIRECTION
1942	70	WATER/4	S	N	E	SE
1954	58	WOOD/1	E	SE	S	N
1966	46	FIRE/7	SW	NW	NE	W
1978	34	EARTH/4	S	N	E	SE
1990	22	METAL/1	E	SE	S	N
2002	10	WATER/7	SW	NW	NE	W

(ie born in 1966 or 2002) do especially those who are able to face the very auspicious direction of West!

Everything that applies to the women also apply to them. The other two categories of Horse men belong to the East group so for them they should use East group directions i.e. North, South, East and Southeast. But in 2012, only two directions are lucky and not afflicted; and facing the other two directions is not advisable. Thus do take note that:

> ▶ **North** is afflicted with illness star; better not to face this direction.
> ▶ **South** is lucky and brings winning energy.
> ▶ **East** brings romance and scholastic luck.
> ▶ **Southeast** is extremely unlucky. Avoid.

IMPROVING HORSE'S FENG SHUI LUCK IN 2012

The fastest way to attract good fortune is to tap your personalized lucky directions. As long as you make certain your lucky direction is not afflicted in 2012, capturing your lucky directions will bring you additional luck that will enhance whatever good fortune may be coming your way. It will also reduce whatever misfortune luck may be lurking in other parts of your chart. If you cannot tap your best direction, you MUST at least avoid facing a direction that is unlucky for you.

Attracting Success

Arrange your work desk so you can sit facing your Success direction. Doing so brings you advancement, growth and enhanced stature in your professional life. Just make sure your Success direction is not afflicted.

For Horse women, note that the West enjoys excellent energy and brings success from feng shui winds but the Southwest is hampered by the hostile star 3 which brings obstacles associated with misunderstandings and also litigations.

Men take note that the Northwest direction is also afflicted in 2012. Here the star of betrayal, burglary and violence is strong so better to avoid it. Sit facing West even if this is not your Success direction and it should bring you winning luck in 2012.

For Horse men whose best direction for advancement is North, you definitely should not use it in 2012 as this is an afflicted direction. Instead, tap into the victory luck of the South direction, as this is the direction that brings success in all your endeavors.

To attract success, arrange your work desk such that you sit facing your *sheng chi* direction. Doing so brings you advancement, growth and enhanced stature in your professional life. But just make sure your *sheng chi* direction is not afflicted this year.

For Horse ladies of the West group, the West direction is the most auspicious for you in 2012, followed by the Northeast. So you have two choices of facing directions. Men belonging to the East group should face South in 2012, as this is clear-cut excellent for you.

> Always make sure that your sitting position is not harmed by physical structures around you such as the sharp edge of a corner, or an exposed overhead beam is above you...

And while arranging your desk to face the direction of your choice, also take note of what to avoid. Always look out for what is behind you. You must make sure never to get hurt by something behind you while focusing on facing your lucky directions. In other words watch your back! So...

- ▶ Avoid having a window behind you, especially if your office or home work area is located several levels up a multi level building. If this is a room on the ground level in your home it is fine.

- ▶ Avoid having the door into your room being placed behind you. It is worse if this is your office at work as talk that is detrimental to you get plotted and planned behind your back. This is a severe taboo.

- ▶ For Horse men belonging to East group, do make sure the door into your office is not facing the Southeast - this would be very unlucky indeed as this is the five yellow direction of this year.

- ▶ For Horses belonging to the West group, make sure the door coming into your office is not facing Northwest or Southwest, even if these two directions are lucky for you. Both these directions are afflicted this year, so using these doors cause problems and obstacles to manifest.

► Avoid being directly in the line of fire of sharp edges or tables, corners and protruding corners. and definitely DO NOT place your desk at funny angles just to tap into your lucky direction. This can backfire bringing misfortune luck instead.

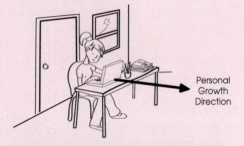

Students Horses should try to tap their personal growth direction if it is not afflicted in 2012. If it is, then try to face another lucky direction based on your Kua. But do NOT have door behind you where you sit. This is very bad and causes others to betray you behind your back.

Ensuring Good Health

An excellent way to ensure good health in 2012 is to capture your individual good health direction. The secret of good health is to sleep with your head pointed to your health direction or at least one of your four auspicious directions. Also ensure your health direction does not suffer from any affliction in 2012.

In this respect, again the Horse women should note that there are two West group directions that are afflicted 2012. These are Southwest and Northwest. So even if this is your personal health (or other good luck) direction, it is advisable to avoid facing these directions in 2012. The Northeast is fine and is in fact auspicious because it enjoys the future prosperity star, so it has connotations of longevity and is thus considered good for health.

As for the Horse gentlemen of the East group, note that North is afflicted by the illness star; so to be on the safe side, it is a good idea to avoid this direction in 2012. Instead face either South or East if you belong to the East group. If you belong to the West group, face West or Northeast. Sleeping right is one of the easiest of feng shui ways to ensure good health.

This plus making certain you are not afflicted by the annual and monthly illness star numbers is what will help ensure you do not succumb to serious illness during the year.

In the Bedroom

To enjoy good feng shui, always be sensitive to the way your bed is oriented and positioned in the bedroom.

CHAPTER 3 : PERSONALISING YOUR FENG SHUI LUCK

A golden rule is that beds should always be positioned against a solid wall, and should not share a wall with a toilet or bathroom on the other side. This gives you the solid support you need and the headboard forms a symbolic protective aura that guards you while you sleep. So it is always preferable to have a headboard.

> You should make sure **never** to have toilets on the other side of the wall where your bed is placed. The toilet symbolically flushes away all bad luck and to have it directly behind you while you sleep suggests that all your good luck gets flushed away as well.

Beds that are placed against a wall with space around it are always more auspicious than beds that are wedged tight into corners. Do make sure there are no heavy beams above you as you sleep and no sharp columns hitting at you from protruding corners and cupboards. These cause illness. And do take note of window views. If you can see blue skies at nights and there is a clear view it is both healthy and auspicious - so also are views of vibrantly growing trees although these should never be too near to your window. But do make sure not to be looking at a dead tree stump or a hostile looking tree outside as these can bring illness into the bedroom.

CHAPTER 3 : **PERSONALISING YOUR FENG SHUI LUCK**

Becoming a Star at School

For the 10 year old Horse teenager, 2012 brings very good Success luck which enables you to perform at full potential. Your all round energy is also good this year so the potential for you to emerge as a star manifests for you in 2012.

What you need to do to harness extra good luck your way is to make sure you sit facing your Personal Growth direction when you are studying at home, working on an assignment, doing your home work or sitting for an examination. Just make sure you are not facing an afflicted direction!

For the boy, your best direction is West and in 2012, this is excellent because the West is so lucky this year. Whatever you do, make sure that you always face West in 2012 when doing any of the important tasks or doing homework.

For the girl, the *Personal Growth* direction is the Northeast which is also very lucky this year so do your work always sitting facing this direction in 2012. Also try to tap Northeast when you sleep as doing so brings the powerful luck of 9 helping you to build strong foundations for your future.

Attracting Romance into your Life

If you are looking for love the good news is that the *peach blossom star* lands in the East in 2012. This is a powerful love direction for activating marriage luck this year. So no matter your age, irrespective of whether you have been married before, this is an excellent year to set the energy moving to bring you good marriage luck.

Those wanting to use this direction to jumpstart their romance luck place a **bejeweled Rabbit** in their East direction! This is excellent for East group ladies. But if you prefer, you can also tap the South direction. Have your head pointing South this year and place a **bejeweled Horse** on your head board or behind your bed as you sleep. This should attract love and romance in to your life.

You can also enhance the energy of marriage luck by using your personalized Love direction based on the Eight Mansions formula, but this must always take account of the afflicted directions. Hence it is better to tap into either West or Northeast for West group Horses ,and East or South for East group. For Horse women, you can also place a **bejeweled Rooster** in the West direction.

Chapter Four

RELATIONSHIP LUCK FOR 2012

The Horse's popularity soars with friends & family alike

Each year, we all react to the people around us differently, and depending on what our sign is, we can be more accommodating in one year and less so in another. How you treat and respond to those you love - your family, lovers, spouse or children - and to those you work with - colleagues, employees, bosses and business associates - depend very much on your relationship energies during the year. This will influence your tolerance levels and your patience. Some years you can be very loving and forgiving, feeling at ease with yourself and with the world, and during other years, you can be less tolerant and very impatient.

CHAPTER 4 : **RELATIONSHIP LUCK FOR 2012**

COMPATIBILITY
WITH EACH ANIMAL SIGN

COMPATIBILITY	LUCK OUTLOOK IN 2012
HORSE with RAT	Strong potency in the arrow of antagonism
HORSE with OX	Fabulous & overflowing with abundance - sum of 10
HORSE with TIGER	A great year for this pair of allies
HORSE with RABBIT	Too much loving so need to cool things
HORSE with DRAGON	Good bonding goes beyond hand holding
HORSE with SNAKE	Keeping each other warm to stay loving
HORSE with HORSE	Finding themselves in a competitive situation
HORSE with SHEEP	Strong ties marred by intermittent hostility
HORSE with MONKEY	A subdued relationship this year
HORSE with ROOSTER	Flying high and making waves together
HORSE with DOG	Allies yes, but divergent interests this year
HORSE with BOAR	Very little affinity between this pair

The Horse sign can be volatile, but this year the Horse is a more subdued creature, full of dreams to win and emerge victorious yet also aware of the afflictions being brought its way. The Horse could become distracted by the *three killings* sitting in its location on the 24 Mountains Compass Wheel, although feng shui winds bring the potential of winning. The energies of the year do not cause the Horse to be difficult in relationships, except that there seems to be little time for socializing.

The Horse has a great deal of patience in 2012 even if it does not appear to have enough leisure time. There is however an overriding attitude of goodwill towards others and there do not appear to be any direct confrontations coming to disturb the Horse's peace of mind.

The Horse personality however can be volatile and moodswings can take their toll on those near and dear to you. Your independence of spirit and the need to take time off to contemplate on what you want to do with your life creates moments when those around you get confused by you. In 2012, your mind seems to be on so many different aspects of your life. Those in middle age will find their thoughts constantly focusing on money-making ventures and on improving your situation whether it be wanting to climb up the career ladder or in a commercially-driven situation. But happily, this distraction away from the various relationships in your life does not get in the way of your interactions with them. You continue to be fairly even-tempered through the year and will be especially warm to those you like.

There is however some tension possible with signs that are in conflict with yours, so there can be some antipathy directed towards your natural astrological "enemy" the Rat sign; but to others, you should have a good store of goodwill.

So if you want it, this is a year when you can have much happiness in your social life. Younger Horses will seek to expand their circle of friends.

The Horse is in its element when it is in a competitive situation. This is a year when its juices are pumping to emerge as the winner - no matter what the scenario of competition may be. But Horses do prefer having familiar people around. They also perform better this way, when those already known to you will feel your charm and warmth coming across more naturally.

CHAPTER 4 : RELATIONSHIP LUCK FOR 2012

Older Horse signs will not be as keen to socialize or to make new friends. But younger members of this sign are keen to seek out adventure and look for new pastures. Horses looking for new thrills will be in their element socializing and showing up at parties even when uninvited. The Horse sign loves going out into the unknown, because here is where its love of the free spirit kicks in.

Animal signs generally interact in a positive way toward their Zodiac allies, secret friends and astrological soulmates. But the extent of affinity does magnify or get reduced according to the feng shui energy of each sign in different years.

So while it is absolutely important to know about these groupings, it is equally important to fine-tune the level of affinity enjoyed each year.

Each sign also has another sign with whom it may be difficult to feel much warmth towards - we call the energy that flow between them arrows of antagonism. It can be troublesome when someone you care for or have just met and feel attracted to belongs to an animal sign that is supposedly your astrological "enemy" - these are signs placed directly opposite you in the Astrology wheel. But like it or not these "arrows" indicate long term incompatibility! The good news however is that astrological antipathy can get reduced when both signs enjoy good fortune years. Or when both have strong inner chi in their chart.

Auspicious Crosses

Having said this, it is always preferred for siblings to be astrological allies, so planning your family according to astrological guidelines does create benefits. There is also an astrological secret associated with "enemy signs" and this gives families the key to unlocking strong lucky vibes for the entire family. This requires the presence of what is generally referred to as the *Auspicious Crosses* formed by four members within a family unit.

These *Crosses* exist in a family when there are two specific pairs of antagonistic siblings, e.g. if you, the Horse also has a Rat, your astrological enemy, in your family, then you have one pair of antagonistic arrows in the family.

But with this pair you can create the highly auspicious Cardinal Cross simply by having a Rabbit and a Rooster also in the family. Then as a unit, your family

CHAPTER 4 : RELATIONSHIP LUCK FOR 2012

FOUR ELEMENT CROSS

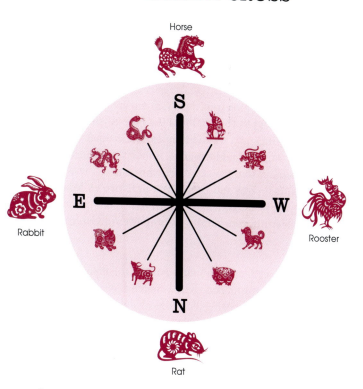

If you have the Four Element Cross in your immediate family, this brings an auspicious vortex of luck, and your arrow of antagonism with the Rat sign then becomes auspicious instead.

will be deemed to have all four elements - Fire, Water, Wood and Metal - and this brings amazing new auspicious flows of energy towards the whole family. Note that for the Cross energies to work, all four of you should be living in the same house and under the same roof.

So for instance for your family, if you are the father or the mother in the family as the Horse, your family unit can create the auspicious Cardinal Cross which comprises a Horse, Rat, Rabbit and Rooster. This requires that you are married to one of these four animal signs and then if you have two children belonging to the other two signs, you would have created within your family a very powerful Cardinal Cross.

So, if in your family you already have the first three signs between you, and there is no end of squabbling between your opposing astrological signs, you can this option in mind.

The Horse's Allies

Your allies are the Tiger and the Dog and in 2012, you will be blessed by an aura of victory. This attracts others to you simply because the world loves a winner and with your allies and your secret friend, the Sheep

ALLY GROUPINGS	ANIMAL SIGNS	CHARACTERISTICS
COMPETITORS	Rat, Dragon, Monkey	Competent, Tough, Resolute
INTELLECTUALS	Ox, Snake, Rooster	Generous, Focused, Resilient
ENTHUSIASTS	**Dog, Tiger, Horse**	**Aggressive, Rebellious, Coy**
DIPLOMATS	Boar, Sheep, Rabbit	Creative, Kind, Emotional

Table above shows Groupings of Allies.

they will naturally gravitate towards you. It benefits your allies to stick closely to you simply because your sign has the good fortune of coming ahead this year.

This is a year when Horse is strong, feeling enhanced by good element indications and by excellent feng shui winds. Horse may not have any special connection with the Dragon Year, but this will not do you any harm. Since Fire is your intrinsic element and there is a shortage of Fire in the year's paht chee chart, you will find that it is you that usually brings good fortune to others.

CHAPTER 4 : RELATIONSHIP LUCK FOR 2012

The Horse's luck is very optimistic and positive. This is a year when you can bring goodwill to many people around you. Your allies have a mixture of good luck and mixed luck.

The Tiger enjoys a good year but the Dog in 2012 is headed for an uncertain time when the winds of fortune blows hot and cold. The Dog sign has a serious affliction in the negative 7 star. This can bring aggravating events or even traumatic loss do it is better to closer to the Tiger than to the Dog in 2012. The Horse benefits from the number 1 star and this suggests that good feng shui winds are blowing your way. The 1 star brings victory and attainment of whatever it is you are working on. There is potential for gains. The Horse has a good store of powerful victory vibes.

Your trinity of allies is thus actually not weak and in fact quite strong in 2012, with the greatest strength being brought by the Tiger who thus plays a big role in the trinity.

In terms of compatibility, the Horse should make real effort to get along with each of your astrological allies, as this lends you strength resulting in better trust and greater friendship with one another.

PAIRINGS OF
SECRET FRIENDS

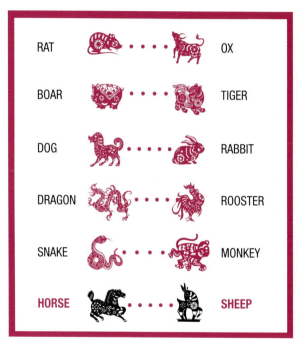

Animal signs that are secret friends are very good
for each other and you can help each other even without knowing.
The Horse's secret friend is the Sheep.

To harness maximum benefit from your affinity allies, it is beneficial to carry the symbolic image of your allies. In 2012, the best for the Horse born is to carry the image of your own sign i.e. the lucky victorious Horse.

You can wear the Horse likeness with confidence because in 2012 this is the **Victorious Horse**. This is best worn as a pendant - as a jewellery item, or you can display the Horse image at work or at home. Inviting the **Horse** into your home brings in the symbolic presence of this wonderful creature.

What will also be great is for you to wear or display your **Allies and Secret Friend Crest** which we have specially designed to place close to you to remind you of their significance in strengthening your energies during the year. The great significance of activating your astrological grouping is often overlooked by many people so do use the **Crest Wallet or brooch** not just to remind you but also to activate the essence of the trinity. For the Horse, what you need is the Crest of the Tiger/Horse/Dog.

The Horse and its allies are known for their amazing courage and great resilience. This is a group of animal signs which display great courage and independence. Together, the three you can achieve much.

Although you each have your own outer and inner strengths, it is the Dog who has the most helpful attitude and the Horse who has the greatest joy of living. The Tiger personality lies somewhere in between. Horse, Tiger and Dog tend to be strong willed and tough, yet they can also be soft and yielding. This is a group of people who are very loyal towards each other and who make good friends, being neither fair-weather nor manipulative. They are thoughtful and sensitive to the needs of the different relationships in their lives.

They are not as competitive as some of the other signs but they can be difficult and stubborn when pushed to the wall or cornered. In 2012 however, the Horse will be quite accommodating. Indeed, in its relationship interactions with its allies, the Horse will be both charming and sensitive. There should not be any problems in the Horse's relationship with either the Tiger or the Dog in 2012.

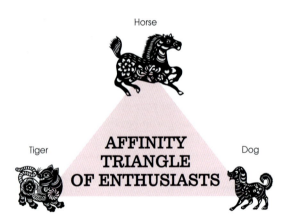

The Horse, Tiger & Dog form an affinity triangle thus there will always be good affinity flowing between you.

(Bringing Out the Best in Each Other ★★★★)

HORSE WITH HORSE
In 2012, finding themselves in a competitive situation

When two people of the Horse sign get together, there instantly ignites a natural born spirit of competition. Unfortunate but true, because in 2012, the Horse is bitten by the wanting-to-win bug. The competitive instincts however are neither hostile nor loud - just two people who would otherwise get along really well treading more carefully around each other. But there is a warm feeling.

What happens between two Horse signs is the recognition of a kindred spirit, for of course, these are people whose attitudes to life are similar and there is also a secret optimism that is infectious. So the mood is pleasant making this a fairly good pairing. The Horse has an attractive personality and being fired up by a competitive streak only makes each come across more interesting.

They should thus have little trouble getting close to one another. The Horse in any case in its natural habitat lives as part of a herd, galloping in packs of hundreds. The Horse is thus a social animal, completely at ease with its own kind. So when these two come together in a partnership or a relationship, we see here a pairing of people with plenty in common. Horse signs are generally outgoing people and in 2012 they continue to be sporty and independent. And while they may not be terribly fired up romance-wise, nevertheless, the Horse is always a romantic and faithful creature.

> As partners, the Horse cooperates well with another Horse. Their ability to work together has roots in shared commitments and similar aspirations; and with the singular lack of jealousy in their makeup despite wanting to outdo one another. This is a great pair to watch as they come to terms with the instincts that arise from wanting shared goals yet wanting to be the greater of two equals.

The secret of their compatibility lies in their expectations of one another being realistic. Much of this is due to their honesty. Horses tend to be highly moral, so this sentiment pervades this relationship. There are no hidden agendas and those living together will rarely be carrying negative baggage. Even when one emerges as a possible leader of the two, the other gives in with the most graceful acceptance.

(*An Ideal Match* ★★★★★)

HORSE WITH TIGER
In 2012, a great year for this pair of allies

The connection between the Horse and Tiger is surreal and their relationship transcends the merely physical, so there is a spiritual dimension to the connection. In many ways, this is a match made in heaven! In 2012 the two signs find magic together. This time however it will be the Horse that will be aggressively pursuing the Tiger, although the big cat will slow down to make sure it gets caught!

> In Horse, Tiger finds a playmate, a fabulous companion and a great business partner. This seems like an ideal match for the brash, loud and adventurous Tiger, because the Horse personality, which closely resembles the Tiger's, is that of a kindred spirit.

These are two people who can easily laugh together, take the Mickey out of each other and still be close, and even take off to the ends of the world should they decide to do so. These kindred souls inspire noble qualities in each other, bringing out the goodness and inner kindness that attracted them to each other in the first place. Communication between the two is intuitive and when together, they share an easy camaraderie and a good sense of humor. This pair is incredibly tolerant of each other and are able to create a world of their own, strongly bonding and staying supportive through life. This match has an excellent chance of lasting long and happy.

They are astrological allies and together with the Dog make up the "three hunters" of the Zodiac. These are people who are unrelentingly patient when stalking their prey, and they inspire in one another the determination to hang in there when the going gets tough. Resilience, courage and determination are some attributes associated with these three signs. They are highly-skilled networkers, able to connect directly with people at any level. They make plenty of friends and few enemies. They are good for each other.

Horse and Tiger are astrological allies and are very good for each other.

(Sharing the Same Humor ★★★★)

HORSE WITH DOG
*In 2012 allies yes,
but divergent interests this year*

These allies of the Zodiac are definitely favorable for one another. Horse and Dog make up a cosy couple who not only enjoy each other's company but also bring out the best things in each other. Between them flows understanding and love.

These two signs find it easy to share ideas and assets and they go through good times and bad with the same spirit of give and take. They also share the same kind of humor and are able to walk through difficult challenges together. They generate powerful synergy to take advantage of whatever opportunities that may open up for them.

They are socially popular and will find that they like the same types of people. The Horse & Dog generate good hype as a couple and as a result, their social life is excellent. Both being extroverts by nature they are good at making friends and transforming business associates into lifelong allies.

Their strength is in networking, making contacts that help them in their work, and in generating goodwill. If they run a business, they work well together.

These are two people who are motivated by high ideals. They cherish the same values, so there is an inner bonding that brings them closer with each passing year. They get fired up and relentlessly pursue causes they believe in. They think alike with neither being overly sensitive nor given to looking to blame the other should things go wrong.

They act out of impulse so there is usually no heavy discussion of serious issues between them. Their interactions are rarely if ever, tensed and they are happy to do away with formality. These are instant decision makers and rightly or wrongly they are quite happy to bumble their way through life, happy to be their own counsel, happy to create their own inspiration.

Horse and Dog go through good times and bad with a good spirit of give-and-take.

The Horse's Secret Friend & Zodiac Housemate

In addition to astrological allies, the Horse also has a Secret Friend and a Zodiac Housemate with whom it creates an incredibly special relationship; one that is even more influential than anything developed with any one of its two allies.

> Sometimes your *Secret Friend* and *Zodiac Housemate* are different signs, but in the case of the Horse sign, your secret friend is *also* your Zodiac Housemate. Thus you will find that you feel exceptionally close to the Sheep sign who not only makes you very happy, this is also your soulmate and probably your best friend too.

As a result, the Horse and Sheep have the potential to forge an extremely close and very compatible relationship. They have a lot of time for one another and there will flow between them quite an exceptional sense of comradeship that generates happiness vibes. Even when they are at odds and disagree, they are still able to stay close. Secret friends nurture one another, bringing out each other's strengths and strong points. It is always beneficial to enter in any kind of relationship with one's secret friend.

CHAPTER 4 : RELATIONSHIP LUCK FOR 2012

As for one's Zodiac's housemate, this likewise generates a flow of hidden strengths and skills. As partners in love, or in business, or as teammates, you can create a powerful alliance which can be very commercially successful. The Horse's Zodiac housemate is the Sheep, and together, they create amazing passion together. This can be a very powerful relationship and they can also bring great luck to one another.

The Horse and the Sheep have a very special realtionship with each other. Not only are they Secret Friends, they are also Zodiac Housemates, forming the House of Passion with each other.

CHAPTER 4 : RELATIONSHIP LUCK FOR 2012

THE 6 DIFFERENT ZODIAC HOUSE PAIRINGS

ANIMALS	YIN/YANG	ZODIAC HOUSE	TARGET UNLEASHED
RAT OX	YANG YIN	HOUSE OF CREATIVITY & CLEVERNESS	The Rat initiates The Ox completes
TIGER RABBIT	YANG YIN	HOUSE OF GROWTH & DEVELOPMENT	The Tiger employs force The Rabbit uses diplomacy
DRAGON SNAKE	YANG YIN	HOUSE OF MAGIC & SPIRITUALITY	The Dragon creates magic The Snake creates mystery
HORSE SHEEP	YANG YIN	HOUSE OF PASSION & SEXUALITY	The Horse embodies male energy The Sheep is the female energy
MONKEY ROOSTER	YANG YIN	HOUSE OF CAREER & COMMERCE	The Monkey creates strategy The Rooster gets things moving
DOG BOAR	YANG YIN	HOUSE OF DOMESTICITY	The Dog works to provide The Boar enjoys what is created

HORSE WITH SHEEP
In 2012, strong ties marred by intermittent hostility

In 2012 the two signs of Horse and Sheep, although astrologically closely linked, could clash with one another. Despite their strong ties, both signs get hit by strongly negative stars brought by the 24 Mountains Compass. The Sheep is sitting on yearly killing stars while Horse is sitting and flanked by *Three Killings* stars.

> It would appear that together or individually they have a lot on their hands. They will need an extraordinary store of patience & goodwill to ride through a stormy 2012. Even with strong feng shui cures in place, it is likely the there will be intermittent hostility causing unhappiness and a great deal of aggravation.

The Zodiac is bullish about a Horse and Sheep pairing as this couple are not just "secret friends" but are also great soulmates as they share the same Zodiac house, that of Sexuality and Passion, with the Horse exuding the male yang energy and the Sheep creating the

(*Intense & Powerful Loyalty* ★★★★)

female yin energy. In Zodiac terms, this translates to suggest complete compatibility. They have a special relationship that is both strong and enduring.

> The Horse and Sheep have the ability to make each other extremely happy. They think in the same way and are physically also very compatible. They are able to please each other and to establish good foundations for long term happiness. Their attraction is rooted in their attitudes which complement each other.

The Horse is forthright and courageous and the Sheep is steady and stable. The Horse also likes to lead and take charge and this too is fine with the gentle and pliable Sheep, although here, the Sheep is the more skilful of the two. Between them is a big store of goodwill and pleasant interchange. There is little cause for conflict and since neither side is of a quarrelsome nature, life in the Horse/Sheep household is peaceful and potentially enriching as well.

If there are any differences between them, these arise from their different attitudes towards child care and upkeep of their children. In this the Horse takes a free spirited approach encouraging independence. The Sheep tends to be more conservative and also less courageous and will tend to stress safety over risk taking. But these differences are easily resolved… especially in 2012 when the Sheep is more likely to have its way.

> **FENG SHUI ADVICE**: It is a good idea to strengthen Horse's immunity to the three killings by placing the **three celestial guardians** in the South and also by placing plenty of Fire energy to subdue the quarrelsome energy of the Southwest. This will ease whatever conflicts erupt between this pair.

The Horse's Astrological Enemy

Astrological feng shui relating to relationships between the twelve animal signs must take note of "astrological enemies". This is represented by the animal sign that directly confronts you on the Compass Wheel.

In the case of the Horse, your enemy is said to be the Rat, so there is usually cross-purpose communication going on between people born of these two signs. Very likely there is also very little in common between these two signs; things can be very trying between you and could even lead to strong quarrels. There is likely to be latent hostility and tensions, unless there is also a Rabbit and a Rooster, in which case the family as a unit forms the Cardinal Cross of animal signs placed in the four Primary directions.

The Cardinal Cross comprises the four elements Wood, Fire, Metal and Water. With all four elements present, the ability to engage the cosmic forces makes for an auspicious phenomenon. Then whatever animosity there is transforms into a potent combination of auspiciousness.

CHAPTER 4 : RELATIONSHIP LUCK FOR 2012

PAIRINGS OF
ASTROLOGICAL ENEMIES

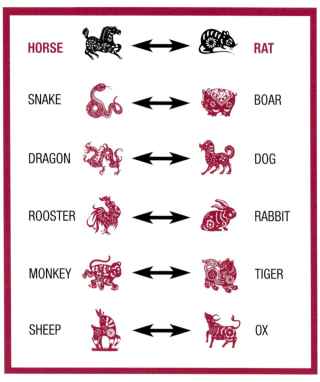

HORSE	⟷	RAT
SNAKE	⟷	BOAR
DRAGON	⟷	DOG
ROOSTER	⟷	RABBIT
MONKEY	⟷	TIGER
SHEEP	⟷	OX

Astrological enemies rarely make good long term partners whether in love or work relationships. Cures must be brought in to improve relations between two astrological foes.

(*Instinctive Animosity Unless Remedied* ★)

HORSE WITH RAT
In 2012, strong potency in the arrows of antagonism

When two animal signs confront each other in the astrological compass, like in the case of the Horse and the Rat, they always suggests the presence of latent hostility. This may not always manifest openly but, it will cause the two personalities to be very short fused and impatient with one another.

From young, the Horse is instinctively wary of the Rat, and if you are in a sibling relationship with a Rat, it is unlikely that you will be very close. In fact, you are likely to be most suspicious of each other. In 2012, a fair bit of this instinctive animosity could surface, with the Rat tending to be very cool to anything said or suggested by the Horse and the latter dismissing the Rat's opinions as "irrelevant".

It does not matter what the nature of your relationship with each other may be; it is a year when animosities manifest and break out in some kind of confrontation.

Should Horse be having difficulties with a Rat spouse, or with a Rat colleague or associate, our advice is for you to understand this and to curb the urge to react negatively should occasion arise for simmering animosity to manifest. Here the problem lies more with Rat, because Rat is easily aggravated this year. There could even be latent animosity and envy of long standing; if you the Horse understands this, it should help you in your interfaces with Rat.

Relationship luck between the two of you can get strained, and can lead to anger and loud voices; but once you understand that this is all part of the astrological roadmap of animal signs, any resentment which might otherwise well up inside you should subside, at least a little.

Note however that arrows of antagonism between zodiac enemies tend to flare up through the year, gaining special potency, so do practice tolerance, especially if you are in a competitive situation with a Rat. As colleagues in a work environment, you might find you have to make extra effort to curb any animosity that may arise.

If you are married to a Rat, and you are feeling in any way dissatisfied, you can comfort yourself and accept that it is not easy to be as close as you want to be; it is also not easy to be understanding or tolerant. It is hard to go too deep with each other not because either is incapable of doing so, but because the inclination to do so just does not exist. In terms of attitudes and character traits, you are as far apart as the North and South pole, with one being Fire and the other being Water.

> Unlike the Rat, the Horse will not put up with the Rat's annoyances even if there is something to be gained from it. If the balance of power in the relationship leans towards the Rat, Horse might well rock the boat.

The Horse is ultimately a free spirit and impulsive and is definitely not as practical as the Rat. So when the situation calls for it, the Horse must subdue whatever hidden resentments may be present. You simply have to try & display a cordial face.

The Horse is less likely to be as clever or as mature as the Rat, and is also a lot more strong willed. In a love relationship, the Rat and Horse couple ignites serious personality clashes. They generate powerful arrows of antagonism towards each other and in 2012, these "clashes of hostility" might well escalate. If it does, it is the Rat who will likely be the one to back off.

CHAPTER 4 : RELATIONSHIP LUCK FOR 2012

The Chinese believe that when a Rat and Horse marry and the marriage lasts, there is potential for great good fortune in the union. This happens if they produce children or add to the family equation a Rooster and a Rabbit. This creates what is known as the *Cardinal Cross*, sometimes also referred to as the *peach blossom quartet*.

When a family comprises the signs of the four cardinal directions, it generates serious good luck. If these four signs are in your paht chee chart, it also indicates great fame and fortune. This is something that is definitely worth considering if you are in this position. In the old days this sometimes prompts families to "adopt" children of certain animal signs to strengthen the feng shui luck of the family.

Horse and Rat can form a most formidable couple if they have a Rooster and a Rabbit child between them.

(*Exhilarating Year for this Pair* ★★★★)

HORSE WITH OX
In 2012, fabulous
& overflowing with abundance

The charismatic Horse steals the heart of the Ox who is very much attracted to the charm of this equine sign. This can well be just a passing phase for the Ox sign, an infatuation so to speak, because the Horse does appear very confident and strong in 2012. But the Ox can also be love with the Horse because there are real sparks between this pair.

The Horse is the *peach blossom* sign of the Ox, so the Horse does inspire intense longing. Unfortunately for Ox in a pairing with the Horse, it is unlikely to be equal in terms of intensity of feelings. It is likely that the Horse will have the upper hand and even call the shots.

The Horse is in a feisty mood this year, changeable, moody and feeling very independent minded. The Ox might find a relationship here quite hard to handle.

The Ox sign suggests someone solid, down-to-earth and pragmatic – not quite the stuff of adventure and romanticism that is so characteristic of the Horse.

CHAPTER 4 : RELATIONSHIP LUCK FOR 2012

In a long term relationship, the intrinsic nature of both cannot be suppressed. So in the same way that Ox might seem rather dour and dull to the Horse, likewise the Ox can also find the Horse's antics a bit much. The Horse will always have a mercurial vitality and an independent nature, unwilling to be tied down and unable to be too disciplined, just the opposite of the Ox. So over time, the differences between them are sure to surface and then difficulties will arise.

But in 2012 there is a whole new feeling to this relationship and happily for the Ox, the Horse is also drawn towards the Ox. This is because of the sum-of-ten configuration in the energy patterns of this pair.

So there will be an exhilarating feeling of climbing mountains and soaring into the skies in search of new worlds to conquer. This is something rare, and with the year bringing such good, balanced chi, truly the sky is the limit for you both.

> If you are a business partnership with the Ox, the year brings good synergy for you both, and if you are in a love relationship, there will develop a mutual respect that will metamorphose into an inner fire. Passion develops and this ignites and sustains you both simultaneously.

The year thus launches Ox into a wild ride, bringing great happiness. With the Horse, the Ox will surely live through an exciting year.

It will be like having a honeymoon time in a relationship. Once you settle into a comfort zone however, cracks could develop in the relationship and these cracks will show mainly because the Ox and Horse were never instant or natural soulmates.

But for the year there is nothing wrong in enjoying the intensity of your relationship. Note here that passion is not necessarily ignited only by physical attraction.

For Ox, the fires of a relationship with a Horse are fuelled more by his/her success aura, because the Horse enjoys much victory luck this year, and if there is anything that turns Ox on, it is success.

Also, as a pair, the sum-of-ten showers some real abundance luck as well. Prosperity luck flows easily to you both and it does appear beneficial to let go and enjoy!

CHAPTER 4 : RELATIONSHIP LUCK FOR 2012

HORSE WITH RABBIT
In 2012, too much loving here; need to cool things.

The Horse and Rabbit are two cardinal signs who can be very good for one another in 2012. In fact, theirs will reflect a mutually productive relationship with both being exceedingly cordial and encouraging. Both signs are well disposed to each other, and there is admiration and respect, although usually from a distance rather than up close.

> Should a relationship develop between this two, inner differences might surface, leaving both sides to wonder if they really have anything at all in common. The Rabbit being so down-to-earth and the Horse being such a free spirit. The Rabbit's attitude to life and living tends to be one of such unwavering stability where security and safe living are carved in stone that the attitude of the Horse is sure to seem bohemian and irresponsible.

The Rabbit is often accused of living life in the bunker, never savoring the wind and rain and hidden from all the greater glories of the environment. At least this is how the Horse would respond to the Rabbit's well ordered life and values. The Horse after

(*Differences May Surface* ★★★)

all has the call of the wild in its bones, a free soul spirit that is unwilling to be tamed.

Adventurous and often foolhardy, the Horse stands for many things the Rabbit does not. One seems far braver and more of a risk taker than the other. So between this pair is a deep divide, so deep that should they live together or get married, hidden tensions could very well surface.

In 2012 there is a great deal of love but also tension in this relationship. The Horse's Fire energy excites and fuels Rabbit's interest, but there is a need to cool things between this pair. If they move too fast, too much loving could cloud their judgement...

The Rabbit must understand that life is one constant battle and the differences with the Horse can prove too fundamental to overcome, and eventually they might need to cool off. The differences between this pair can be quite insurmountable. In their journey through life, one cannot have a hundred percent trust. This becomes a big problem for them.

CHAPTER 4 : **RELATIONSHIP LUCK FOR 2012**

HORSE WITH DRAGON
In 2012, good bonding goes beyond handholding

Should these two signs get together, they are in for a very interesting year, for the Horse and Dragon have a mutually productive/exhaustive relationship which is both mesmerizing and draining at the same time.

> This relationship with the Dragon is on balance a middling kind of pairing that has the potential to rise to great heights, and in 2012, the Horse will try to take them high high higher! This reflects the Horse's heightened horse power in 2012, a year when the urge to win and fly and soar and drive itself to excellence is in top gear.

The trouble is that Dragon does not have enough energy to be in the mood for too much climbing especially to new heights. Dragon simply lacks the Life Force, the energy and worst of all, it lacks the inner Chi Essence which this kind of competitive living needs. So in 2012, should Dragon want to bond with the Horse, it will mean going beyond handholding!

Getting into a love or business relationship with the Horse can turn out to be a lot more than what the dragon bargains for. There is excitement and there is victory, but there is also danger and the magnified

(*Mezmerizing But Draining* ★★★)

affliction of the *three killing*s. This is a year when the Horse lives dangerously, and for the Dragon, already afflicted by the five yellow, it would seem rather unwise to flirt with dangerous scenarios.

This coupling brings two very magnetic people together. This is a couple with Fire and Wind, speed and strength; strong clashes and equally powerful passion. There won't be any kind of animosity because both are so egotistical and neither feels any inferiority to the other. Here it is more of a situation where two dynamic free spirits learn to adjust and adapt. Those able to transcend their differences will have a thoroughly enjoyable and passionate love affair. Those who cannot maintain the pace could fall by the wayside. Should this pair marry, it must be a love match, as anything arranged is doomed from the start. They are too headstrong to generate the required patience of living together unless they already care for each other.

The Horse sets a big store by love and loyalty and it simply assumes that its mate will go with it to the ends of the world. The Dragon can also be sufficiently romantically inclined to get carried away by the passion of the moment, but in 2012, it is good to slow down, and to think carefully before plunging into too many new adventures!

CHAPTER 4 : RELATIONSHIP LUCK FOR 2012

HORSE WITH SNAKE
In 2012, keeping each other warm by staying loving

These two signs, Horse and Snake can create good bonding in 2012, with the Horse giving the Snake a much needed helping hand to overcome the challenges of the year but getting into a serious love relationship will take time. Or it might not happen at all.

> These are attractive Fire element people who can get intense with one another; but while the Horse tends to be overtly fiery and passionate, the Snake is cool and calm, much better at keeping its fires well under control. Their differences are thus obvious.

These two signs live to different rhythms; and their heartbeats vibrate to different tunes. The Horse may be the *peach blossom animal* of the Snake, but there is little to spark off an immediate romance between them. The Horse could well come across as too much of a free spirit, too independent and adventurous for the genteel Snake. But in 2012, Horse has much to offer beleaguered Snake. Despite sitting on the star of three killings brought by the 24 Mountains Compass,

(*Passion Might Take Time* ★★★)

the Horse is strong and vibrant in 2012, and it is a victorious Horse we are dealing with.

> In this Year of the Dragon, the Horse breathes new life into its own psyche and is determined to leapfrog into a new league. The Snake is drawn to this show of strength.

In 2012, the Snake will respond to overtures sent out by the Horse and although in matters of the heart the Snake would not usually respond to the Horse, this year, they can become an item without too much encouragement. Should they get together as a couple or if they are married, the year 2012 will see the Horse being strong for the Snake, and successfully providing a much-needed shoulder.

It is a happy situation for this pair as the Snake shows its appreciation; and this positive response to the Horse brings out its other qualities and attributes. And so the pair embark on a lovely cycle of love. Horse can be as sophisticated as Snake desires, but the essence of the Horse soul is a freedom and independence unfettered by convention.

In 2012, these qualities of the Horse do not stand in the way of a real relationship being forged between the two signs. But how long it can sustain is something else.

Horse signs tend to be chattier than Snake signs, so there could be mismatched perceptions that cause misunderstandings about depth of feelings and superficiality of responses. The Snake can be as superficial as sliced bread or as deep and likewise the Horse. But unless this pair can develop an easy and relaxed feeling of respect between them, any relationship they forge will be at best lukewarm.

Horse and Snake are two Fire signs that can work well together despite their personality differences.

(Can Complement Each Other ★★★)

HORSE WITH MONKEY
A subdued relationship

The Horse is quite an unlikely match for the Monkey, and in 2012, any coming together of this pair will be quite subdued and low key. These are two of the Zodiac's most mesmerizing signs. They have distinctly strong and noisy personalities but are somewhat intimidated, one by the other.

Physically, these two signs could not be more different. Temperamentally too, they are very unlike each other, and merging them into a couple is quite an impossible task. It would be like trying to merge the wind with the sun.

The Horse can be as fast as a furiously blowing wind or as gentle as a light morning breeze. The Monkey is the sun, radiant, brilliant and glowing with its bright intellect and its incredible cunning. Yet to describe them as diametrical opposites would not be doing them justice. Indeed they can well complement each other beautifully if there were sparks of love to act as a catalyst, otherwise any relationship between this pair will be low key and eventually even fizzle out.

What brings them together and makes them compatible are the similarity of their expectations – from their aspirations of life, from friends, colleagues and from each other! These are natural leaders, able to lead battalions into the field of battle. They have charisma and strong tough energy levels. But the way they go about achieving their goals differ substantially.

The Horse is a super charged machine ready to fly at a moment's notice. The Monkey is more cunning and will always think things through. One is impulsive and the other cautious.

In 2012, it is the Horse who has the edge on winning, making something successful and turning impulsive action into glorious virtue. Monkey tends to be quarrelsome and so will be less effective than Horse.

Should they discover each other in 2012, this pair could love each other to death, for one will inspire the other to great heights. In this pairing, the Horse brings a natural vitality that is endearing to the Monkey and in 2012, the Monkey is all set to plunge into new ventures. There is a sense of expectation for them both which is addictive and exhilarating. So the

CHAPTER 4 : **RELATIONSHIP LUCK FOR 2012**

potential exists then for a low key and rather subdued relationship to soar and fly!

All that is needed is for the Horse and Monkey to work out how best to combine their respective strengths without succumbing to too many disagreements. Monkey needs to stay cool and Horse needs to curb its enthusiasm.

The Monkey and Horse pair works well together as long as there is genuine passion and love.

HORSE WITH ROOSTER
In 2012, flying high & making waves together

The Horse might find it hard to keep up with the feisty and no-nonsense Rooster who is on a roll in 2012. Indeed, while Horse is ambitious and raring to go, the erstwhile bird is also super-charged, as energies and inner Chi Essence reach red hot levels.

Both Horse and Rooster benefit greatly from the white stars bringing good fortune to their locations; the Horse with the winning 1 and the Rooster with the auspicious 8, so a pairing of these two signs in 2012 is expected to be very fruitful indeed.

But how far they can take their good energy together depends on how well they work together. Here, Horse will find it something of a challenge to keep up with Rooster.

These two signs have an amazingly cordial relationship considering how different they are, and can be. In 2012, their energy levels are at different levels. The normally energetic and vibrant Horse is not operating at peak capacity, while the Rooster on

(*An Unconventional Synergy* ★★★)

the other hand enjoys a very high energy year. Inner chi essence of the Rooster is also at its peak. Usually for any couple to enjoy a love relationship or flourish in a business partnership, their energy levels should be balanced so neither leaves the other lagging, unless one is so strong as to lift the other up as well.

In 2012, the Rooster's Life Force and Spirit Essence are at their peak enabling the already strong and domineering Rooster to simply take charge. If this issue can be settled amicably between the pair, then Horse and Rooster have a reasonable chance of enjoying a good time together in this Year of the Dragon. This acceptance of each other's role, with the Rooster in command of the relationship, opens very exciting and positive avenues for the couple to work and live together. As long as Horse accepts Rooster dominance, the year works well for them.

The Horse becomes surprisingly adaptable in 2012 in all likelihood because it appreciates the value of the Rooster and can recognise that he/she is able to blend in with Rooster's conventional approach to making things happen. In a marriage then, this is a couple which can make it together. In many ways, the synergy created is unconventional, but there is genuine appreciation underlying this relationship. Hence it works.

HORSE WITH BOAR
In 2012, very little affinity between this pair

There is simply too little working in favor for this pair. In 2012 these two signs live their lives at completely different rhythms. The Horse is an instant sort of person, action-oriented and often impulsive. The Boar on the other hand tends to be plodding and careful, rarely jumping into action the way the Horse does.

So do not expect there to be any instant attraction between this two. Having said that, this does not mean a pairing between this couple cannot work. If they somehow end up with one another, it is quite possible for them to be moderately happy together, taking pride in appreciating each other's qualities and often good-naturedly seeing the other in a positive light.

They are comfortably undemanding of one another and are able to maintain a happy absence of formality between them. Discussions between them are always civil, and since both believe in enjoying the best of life's many indulgences, they are quite happy to be a little irresponsible about money and other material issues. The Boar is easily content as long as his/her domestic life is undisturbed and they are financially secure.

(*Providing Support but Lacking Passion*)

Both signs will not be overtly ambitious, even if individually or in other situations they are or can be. But together they will live a rather uninspiring life with neither one being consumed by any burning determination to be the biggest, greatest or first in whatever they do, being perfectly happy to maintain their domestic equipoise.

This is not to suggest a total lack of aspirations. As a couple, they will be surprisingly strong together, each providing the other with valuable support. Should they be confronted challenges, they do not necessarily walk away. But this pairing lacks the passion that Horse can generate with some other sign.

In 2012, Boar gets hurt by the number 7 star, so Boar could become the victim of betrayals or experience some kind of loss. This makes Boar less keen to take unnecessary risks or be as brave as the Horse. As a result, they will tend to vibrate to different rhythms.

Chapter Five

ANALYZING HORSE'S LUCK FOR EACH MONTH IN 2012

The Horse born can look to a wonderful year ahead! You enjoy fresh new opportunities that will go a long way in building your confidence. Obstacles and barriers disintegrate, making anything you choose to pursue much easier. Success comes easily, especially in competitive situations. You enjoy victory luck and can emerge triumphant on most occasions. Your main affliction to worry about this year is the Three Killings star, which flies into your sector; so make sure you have your three celestial guardians in the South to ensure this does not become a problem for you. Overall, the Year of the Water Dragon promises to bring much success and contentment to the Horse.

CHAPTER 5 : ANALYSING YOUR LUCK IN EACH MONTH

FIRST MONTH
February 4th - March 5th 2012

YEAR BEGINS BEAUTIFULLY SUM-OF TEN-LUCK BRINGS GOOD NEWS

The Horse gets off to a great start, with a fulfilling month to look forward to. There is indication of fabulous completion luck in your chart. Projects and undertakings started much earlier start to come together and you see your efforts bearing fruit. It is a fast-paced month, and that's just the way you like it. In fact, it seems that the more frenzied the pace, the more you get done. Career luck is excellent and you have every chance to leap ahead. As for your love life, it positively sizzles! Just be careful you don't wear yourself down with piling too much on your plate. Remember to pace yourself!

WORK & CAREER - Beware Scandal

There's plenty happening at work this month, but if you're finding your job stimulating and rewarding, you won't mind a bit putting in extra long hours or working the occasional weekend. Some of you may even start to mix work with pleasure, and while this could spell the start of a beautiful romance for some of you, it could also point to scandal and trouble for others of you. Be careful when playing with fire. Small infidelities can get out of hand quicker than you imagine. The Horse is a playful creature, and when led on, will reciprocate with as much if not more passion. But at heart you are incredibly loyal and moral, so don't let a misstep spoil things for you. The damage could be professional as well as personal.

BUSINESS - Popularity Luck

A good month to become decidedly more high profile. You enjoy popularity luck this month, and Horses in the limelight do especially well. This is a time to step up meetings with the press and media. Plan launches of new products and big announcements for this month. The Horse in business is truly in its element. Be creative with new directions in which you expand and diversify. You are feeling quite ingenious, but more importantly, you have the good luck to back you up and to help ensure the decisions you take are good ones. This is also a good time to spend some effort networking; the contacts you make now could prove invaluable in the near future.

LOVE & RELATIONSHIPS - Passionate

A positively brilliant month when your dreams, and desires are all within your reach! Whether you are looking to expand your network of friends or deepen particular relationships, you are armed with the charm and charisma to do so. Your wonderful sense of humor comes to the fore, and keeping others entertained comes naturally to you. A great month to propose, get engaged or get married.

> Single Horses will very much enjoy attention from the opposite sex this month, and someone extremely interesting could make an appearance in your life soon. Don't let a busy work schedule deter you from having some personal time to socialize. If you plan your time well, there is no reason why both your work and love life cannot thrive at the same time.

EDUCATION - Exhilarating

The month ahead looks hectic but exhilarating for the young Horse. Your energy levels are up – not something too common for the Horse this year – so make the most of it to get ahead in the classroom. This is your chance to make an impression. Don't be afraid to look stupid. Everyone loves just about anything you say. As long as you don't try too hard to impress, it will be hard for others not to be impressed with you. Such is your fabulous luck this month.

CHAPTER 5: ANALYSING YOUR LUCK IN EACH MONTH

SECOND MONTH
March 6th - April 4th 2012

AUSPICIOUS FENG SHUI WINDS CONTINUE

The wealth star flies into your chart, carrying on the great momentum started last month. This is one of your luckiest months this year, so don't waste it. You're on a roll and as long as you keep letting the ideas flow, you'll stay impressively productive. Others flock to your natural magnetism and you'll have no shortage of good company. And the more contact you have with others, the more switched on you'll become. But don't garner knowledge for no reason; put it to good use. Focus on connecting all the dots, and the big picture will crystallize in your head. If you need to improve your financial situation, look at how you can make more and spend less. If it's love you are after, pursue it determinedly. You enjoy luck on all fronts this month, so look on this as a time to conquer the world, and you most definitely can.

WORK & CAREER - Making Great Progess

A great time to look ahead at your career path before you. You could move to a new level in your job, and some of you will even enjoy a promotion. Don't make a pay raise or a fancy title your ultimate goal; look beyond that. Even if your name card, salary and position stay unchanged, valuable strides could be made that augment your importance within the company. Stay long term in your goals, and your eventual prize will be much bigger and more worthwhile. Keep your eyes and ears open to new opportunities. Get to know everyone you're working with intimately. Go beyond the scope of your job. The more useful you make yourself, the more indispensable you'll become; and the day will come – sooner rather than later - when you exceed even your own wildest ambitions.

BUSINESS - Things Going Your Way

Business luck is excellent this month. A good time to start new projects, sign agreements, join up with a promising partner or launch a new product. A great time to engage in important discussions or to pitch for a lucrative contract. Things go your way this month and others are attracted to your good Chi. You work well in a partnership or team situation, and also make a good leader right now. Wear the **Fire Totem Talisman Pendant** to give power to your speech. You have many great ideas to share, and using some feng shui help will ensure your ideas get received just the way you intended. If you need to approach someone for a favor, this is the time to do so. It is hard to say no to the Horse this month. But while you may be feeling successful and quite invincible, don't dismiss opinions and ideas from others. Stopping to listen will give you a more cohesive picture of the situation, allowing you to make better and more informed decisions.

LOVE & RELATIONSHIPS - Popular
You get on great with everyone you meet, potential suitors included. The single Horse in search of a mate will most likely be in no shortage of admirers right now. But you are such an amiable character, that the special someone you have your eye on may not even know, since you seem to get along with everyone equally well. If you like someone, make a real effort to let it show. Go out on a limb if you have to and seal the deal before the month is up and your fabulous luck dissipates.

Make your move and lose your inhibitions. You won't come out sounding like a fool unless you feel like one. And even then, that is no bad thing, as others seem to enjoy you however you present yourself. This month holds many good things in store for you. But you can't have everything, so be sure of what you want, then go for it.

THIRD MONTH
April 5th - May 5th 2012

BE ALERT TO FAIR WEATHER FRIENDS; DON'T BE TOO TRUSTING

After a stellar two months, this month could be a rude awakening. The violent #7 star makes an appearance in your chart, bringing dishonest people into your life. It also brings risk of loss and risk of being cheated. Make sure you have your feng shui cures in place. Have the **double horned rhino** and **6 tusk elephant** in the South of your home, and carry the **Blue Rhino hanging** with you to keep you safe while out and about. This is no month to be taking risks. Keep a low profile and lie low. Lady Horses should beware snatch thieves and avoid staying out too late at night. The energies have turned hostile and thus you should be prepared. Blue and blacks are good colors to wear to counter the aggressive sword energies of the month.

Place the Rhino and Elephant pair in the South of your home to counter the robbery star in your home sector this month.

WORK & CAREER - Office Politics

When the *loss star* pays a visit, you stand at risk of being cheated or betrayed, even by those you consider friends. Don't be too trusting. This month it is better to play your cards close to your chest. Don't reveal everything and don't be too honest. Stay on your guard and watch your back. Office politics could rear its ugly head, and you could be ill prepared with things having gone so smoothly in the recent past.

Display a **Rooster** on your workdesk to protect yourself from becoming a victim of politicking at the workplace. You may need to put in more work than usual, and spend more time double checking your work. Mistakes made now are not so easily forgiven, and could get blown out of proportion. Don't let one bad month set you back. Be meticulous with your work and don't give anyone a reason to criticize you.

BUSINESS - Lie Low; Keep Watch

This month doing less could get you further. Do not try to interfere with the systems too much. If something ain't broke, don't fix it. This is no time to be changing direction or having a massive change in strategy. Maintain the status quo and stay out of any politicking among the staff. Try not to take sides; you don't want to appear to favor some over others. Things may not be what they seem; employees who seem trustworthy could turn out to be not, and vice versa. Keep a closer watch on the money side of things. If people know you are checking, they will be less tempted to help themselves to what is not theirs. Avoid investing and risk-taking this month. This period favors planning and strategizing, rather than moving forward. Save the implementation of new ideas for next month.

LOVE & RELATIONSHIPS - Prickly

You have little success when it comes to romantic situations this month. Things you say or do may be taken the wrong way. Not the best of times to pursue a new relationship. For those of you in steady relationships, things could get prickly between you and your partner. But while you may need your space from each other, don't make too much space or there is danger that one or both of you could end up in the arms of someone else, leaving much to regret later on. Wear the **anti-infidelity amulet** to protect your relationship from harm from third party interference. Try to be more giving in the relationship. Things are bound to improve next month.

CHAPTER 5: ANALYSING YOUR LUCK IN EACH MONTH

FORTH MONTH
May 6th - June 5th 2012

GOOD FORTUNE SMILING ON YOU; HO TU COMBINATION BRINGS SUCCESS

You not only have the heaven star pay a visit, it forms a *Ho Tu* combination in your chart, bringing fabulous success luck your way! Things go magnificently for you. This is a time to make the most of your good luck indications by seizing whatever opportunities come your way. You can take risk, invest, make important decisions… all with confidence this month, because you have luck on your side. You also enjoy good mentor luck, so do take the advice of older and wiser people this month. This is also a promising time for the young Horse looking for direction. Use this opportunity to push yourself beyond your limits. This will help launch you off a plateau you may feel you have reached, taking you to new and greater heights.

WORK & CAREER - People Helping You
There are people in powerful places helping you, whether directly or behind the scenes. Being on the good side of your boss is your key to success this month. Work closely with your superiors. Don't let

them forget you exist because out of sight is out of mind when it comes to promotion time. If you want to ensure you are not left out, be a little more pushy and forthcoming. Learn to be a political animal if that's what's required in your job.

If you are offered the opportunity to take on more responsibilities this month, do so. This is your one chance to really stand out from the rest. It is worth slogging it this month, for your hard work can ripen into a promotion or a better paycheck. Don't waste the opportunity if it is offered to you.

BUSINESS - Good Time to Network

You may be thinking of expanding your business or your workforce. A good friend may come to mind, but beware when hiring friends for you risk jeopardizing your friendship. Think through all the possibilities before employing a buddy. It may be better to work on contract or freelance basis if you want to help out a friend this way.

This is a good time to brush up your own skills in certain areas. You may have specialists in various divisions of your business, but there is nothing like knowing your own operations intimately. Even if you are not directly involved on a day-to-day basis, make it a point to know what is going on. This is also a great time to network more aggressively. Many doors will open for you if you know the right people.

LOVE & RELATIONSHIPS - Magical
Your love life is really quite magical this month! If you already have your eye on someone, this is the time to turn on the charm. You have the good fortune to be able to pick and choose your mate, so if you are not already attached but thinking about settling down, think carefully. Some of you may be weighing the options. If you can't decide between two people, perhaps you just haven't met the right person yet. When the magic moment comes, you will know it. Married Horses are also in for a good month when you enjoy some unforgettably intimate moments with your spouse.

EDUCATION - Mentor Luck
A fabulous month lies ahead for the young Horse. You do well in your studies and have great rapport with your teachers. Spend time developing relationships with those who can help you in your scholastic career. You are enjoying excellent mentor luck and having a mentor figure in your life right now is the best way for you to make some truly impressive progress.

FIFTH MONTH
June 6th - July 6th 2012

GETTING HOT UNDER THE COLLAR AS PRESSURES BRING MISFORTUNE

Your luck takes a nosedive and obstacles start to show themselves. Don't make a big deal when things don't quite go as planned. When you give too much energy to obstacles and difficulties that arise, they become even more insurmountable. Your problems will be short-lived, so don't let anything dampen your spirits too much. Look on this as a time to consolidate and plan for the future.

Take a short holiday if you need one to recharge. Those of you who have been living life in the fast lane probably badly need a vacation. There will be wet blankets along the way pouring cold water on your enthusiasm. Don't pay too much attention to people out to make you feel down. You have rivals and their motives are not in your best interests. Surround yourself only with people who make you feel good about yourself. You may be emotionally more fragile than usual; call on the support of family and good friends if you feel the need. They will be there for you.

WORK & CAREER - Tread Carefully

This is an inauspicious month, so it is important to watch your step. Try not to be overly forceful when dealing with others. While you are looking to get your own way, making progress at the expense of others will only backfire in the end. Don't let emotions cloud your judgment when it comes to work. And don't take anything personally. Sure there may be one or two who don't have your best interests at heart. But it is not personal. Play smart if you want to preserve all the good work you have put in thus far.

Others may find it difficult relating to you because you read too much into everything that's said and done. Don't allow your moody disposition to create a rift between yourself and others. The last thing you need right now is to be alone. Try to see the positive side of everything said to you. If there are none, ignore the comments and don't let it affect you. But try to see the difference between constructive criticism and straight-out put-downs. If you refuse to improve yourself, you could find your job in jeopardy.

BUSINESS - Be Eloquent

You may be finding it challenging to communicate your ideas effectively to others this month. There could be differences of opinion making cooperation between key players difficult or even impossible. Avoid acting on rumors. Make sure you have the whole story before taking any action. Ignorance is your weak link this month, but as long as you know this you can do something about it. When communicating, try and be more eloquent; otherwise do not blame your staff for not following orders.

LOVE & RELATIONSHIPS - Quarrelsome

Silly fights with your partner or spouse could leave you feeling sorry for yourself. When you disagree over an issue, calm yourself and reflect at the problems at hand before insisting the other person is in the wrong. Try to outline everything objectively. Avoid taking things personally. It may be better to give in if there's an issue you can't resolve. Learn to laugh things off and you won't feel so bad when your partner inadvertently says something offensive.

EDUCATION - Ask For Help If You Need It

You may hit some learning barriers this month. Don't get overly frustrated if you don't get something the first time. Working in study groups may help. While at times doing your own reading will suffice, you may find you have to do more this month if you want to really get on top of your work. Ask for help if you need it.

SIXTH MONTH
July 7th - Aug 7th 2012

BACK TO THE DRAWING BOARD; A TIME TO STRATEGISE

Things improve drastically for the Horse this month, so you have plenty to look forward to! Ideas start to flow again and you find easy solutions to problems that seemed insurmountable just a short while ago. It is as if a great weight has been lifted off your shoulders. Enjoy the lightness of the month! The number 4 star has flown in, while the misfortune star has flown out. This brings romance and relationship luck to the fore. Your bristly encounters of last month sort themselves out, and foes become friends again. This is a good month also for young Horses in school, and for those of you pursuing literary or scholastic pursuits. Enjoy a creative and productive four weeks ahead!

WORK & CAREER - Beware Temptation

Beware amorous temptation at the workplace. A new colleague could catch your eye in the romantic sense. But it is a terrible idea to start something up with a co-worker if you are serious about a future in your current job. Keep your personal life out of the office.

There may be other non-romantic complications in relationships with colleagues this month. Don't make firm commitments now, as you may have to break them. The best way to make the most of the next four weeks is to direct your passion into producing really excellent work. This will get you noticed by those who matter, bringing you closer to that promotion you are after. It will also keep you out of trouble.

BUSINESS - Spend Time Planning

For the Horse in business, this is a time to strategize. You are feeling creative and have many exciting new ideas. While you may be itching to implement some of these new ideas, this month is better spent planning than forging ahead impulsively. Brainstorming sessions can be invaluable at this time; use them to develop good ideas into ones which are practical and easily applied. You also enjoy terrific relationship luck, so work these energies to your advantage. Your superior interrelationship skills could win you a lucrative contract or two. Keep a relatively high profile so that when people are looking for someone to approach with an opportunity, they remember you. Friendships may conjure up unexpected business opportunities. Have a listen because it could make you some good money.

LOVE & RELATIONSHIPS - Too Amorous

This month you are absolutely lucky in love! If you are single, you are likely the center of attention and loving every moment of it. But this month is more about physical passion than emotional connecting. Not necessarily the best of times to enter into a new steady relationship or you could jump straight out of it again. While the single Horse will enjoy playing the field, married Horses have to be a bit careful. The *amorous star* could play havoc with your life, bringing third party interference into your marriage. If you sniff out something suspicious, snuff it out immediately. Don't leave your spouse with your best friend, and don't encourage or even allow one-on-one dinners between your other half and a sweet young thing. You're not being paranoid; you're being smart.

EDUCATION - Brilliant Month for Students

A great month when it comes to any scholastic pursuits. The student Horse will find him or herself creative, clever and popular with the class. This is also a good time to work in teams or groups, and to make a good impression on examiners, teachers and anyone who matters. Enhance study and exam luck with the **Chi Lin with 4 Scholastic implements** in the South of your study room.

CHAPTER 5 : ANALYSING YOUR LUCK IN EACH MONTH

SEVENTH MONTH
Aug 8th - Sept 7th 2012

HOSTILITY & MISUNDERSTANDINGS BRING TENSION

The month ahead is characterized by conflicting opinions and opposing views. All this makes you irritable and more easily riled. You may find it difficult to decide things for yourself, but at the same time you're unlikely to take kindly to others holding a divergent view from your own. Don't allow yourself to get stuck in a rut being indecisive. Leave the big decisions till another time. For the small things, tell yourself it doesn't matter what you decide either way. But if you ask others for their opinion, learn to listen. And think before you speak to avoid offending others.

WORK & CAREER - Quarrelsome

Your quarrelsome mood follows you to the workplace, making you difficult to work with. Misunderstandings with co-workers could make this is stressful month at work. Stop yourself when you find you are disagreeing just to be difficult. Sometimes you may disagree out of habit, and this will make you really difficult to work with. Snap out of it before someone of importance

CHAPTER 5: ANALYSING YOUR LUCK IN EACH MONTH

notices. If you are in a competitive environment at work, others may leapfrog you this month. Make an extra effort to be more patient. Don't let your temper get the better of you, and don't lose your cool. This month is better spent working quietly on your own than engaging in too many discussions. Constantly step back to take in the big picture or your work quality will suffer.

BUSINESS - Legal Aggravations

If there are any contracts or agreements to sign, make sure you have a good lawyer working for you, or you could miss something. This is a month when lawsuits and litigation may cause you some aggravation. If you can help it, avoid fighting in court this month. Schedule hearings in a month where your luck is strong. This month your luck is weak and the stars in your chart are making you more quarrelsome and less rational than usual. You need to protect your business this month, particularly if you are operationally very active. Display a **Kuan Kung with Five Dragons** prominently in your office, and display the **Pi Yao with Red Sword** in the South sector.

LOVE & RELATIONSHIPS - Relax

Your love life cools down mostly due to your short fuse. Don't take yourself too seriously. Your touchy temperament is what is driving others away. If you have someone willing to put up with your moods and your bad temper, don't let them go. Don't drive them away by rejecting their overtures; someone has to be the one to dissipate the tension, and if you are lucky enough to find someone who will do it for you, rejoice and let them help you!

EDUCATION - Learn to Listen

Don't get frustrated if you cannot get everything perfect on first try. The more particular you are, the less chance you have of actually completing assignments on time. You are more concerned this month about having your say than listening to others. But if you really want to learn, listening is the best way to go.

EIGHTH MONTH
Sept 8th - Oct 7th 2012

AUTUMN WINDS BRING THE SNIFFLES - ILLNESS ENERGY PREVAILS

The illness star flies in, putting you at risk of falling sick and meeting with accidents. Not a good month to be overly active physically. Those of you who pursue sports that may be dangerous should take extra care this month. You may be slowed down by headaches and other aches and pains this month. A lack of sleep could also be weakening your immune system. Take your health seriously. If you come down with something this month, even a trivial illness could take a long time to cure. While not life-threatening, catching ill now would most certainly slow you down. For some of you, this could mean the difference between a promotion and staying where you are at work. To be productive this month, you're going to need to hold on to your good health.

WORK & CAREER - Average

Career luck is very average this month. Your job may start to feel monotonous, and going to work each day could start to feel like a real chore. A large part of the reason could be your health. If you are feeling poorly, you will hardly be up to the task of staying chirpy throughout the workday. Devise a schedule where you make best use of your time. Don't come home late every night. Even if you may be feeling strong, too many late nights will almost certainly take their toll on you. You are far better off working smart than working hard. Look for shortcuts rather than plodding on and on. Next month you will start seeing the light at the end of the tunnel, and clarity of thought returns.

BUSINESS - Take It Easy

Your difficulty in focusing and making sound decisions this month suggests that this is a good time to go on holiday and let your business run itself for a while. If you're a one-man-show, you'll welcome some help this month. You may consider hiring some part-timers, particularly if you are in an industry where business speeds up as you approach year-end.

When things happen that surprise you, refrain from reacting immediately. Think things through before responding to a crisis if you want to make the best decisions possible. Don't shoulder your problems alone. Give your key staff and managers more responsibilities and they could surprise you with their competency.

LOVE & RELATIONSHIPS - Comfortable

Horses in steady relationships find they have a comfortable rapport with their partners. This month is more about gentle loving than sizzling passion and bedroom activity. You enjoyed being pampered and looked after, especially if you're feeling sickly or poorly. If your partner is the sort to give in to you, you will feel right at home this month.

Even single Horses prefer cozy nights in than wild nights on the town, and this will likely influence your taste in company right now. As romance is low on your list of priorities, this month you may well enjoy developing and deepening your bonds with platonic friends and acquaintances.

HEALTH - Be More Careful

This month the number 2 star brings illness but also risk of accidents, so be careful when participating in rough sports, and don't drive too fast. Carry a **protective talisman** to keep you out of harm's way and make an extra effort to avoid risks. Don't get into cars of drivers known to be reckless or fool hardy. You can't afford to take chances like that this month. If embarking on long-distance car journeys, make sure you don't drive when you are tired or sleepy.

NINTH MONTH
Oct 8th - Nov 6th 2012

A MONTH OF DOUBLE VICTORY LUCK

What a wonderful month for the Horse! You enjoy victory luck doubled and competitive pursuits are met with much success. You're raring to go and relish nothing better than a challenge. If you've been stuck in some kind of rut, this month you can pick yourself and bounce right out of it. If you have been pursuing something with little success, try a different approach. Sometimes that's all it takes; a little tweak to get things moving again.

Some of you will experience a meaningful transformation. Horses with lofty ambitions can embrace the opportunities that come your way. Make an effort to keep up with all the contacts you've made through the year. One day soon you may need to call on some help. Some Horses will be given the chance to assume a leadership position, whether at work or within society. Take it. Good fortune luck is supporting you and chances are you will make a big success of it. Display the **Victory Horse** in the South sector and carry your **Crest of Allies** to boost your good luck this month.

WORK & CAREER - Forging Ahead

There's no stopping the Horse in pursuit of a hotshot career. This month you are on fire and have victory luck on your side. Go after that promotion with gusto if that is what you want. For others of you, you might be headhunted and offered a new opportunity. Think carefully before making an important life-changing decision like changing jobs. Chances are you are doing well in your current situation. Go with your heart if you're undecided. You may have to take a leap of faith, but do so with confidence and a positive attitude.

BUSINESS - Exciting New Opportunities

The Horse in business has much to look forward to. You make a motivational boss and leader, so schedule in time with your staff and those who work for you. You are gur a strong case and can get anyone to come around to your way of thinking, making this also a good month for important discussions and negotiations. Wear the popularity scarf with special mantra to hone the effectiveness of your speech. The pen is mightier than the sword, and your words are mightier than the pen right now. A good time to invest and to expand. When new opportunities make their way to you, take the trouble to check them out. You could land yourself something very big this month. Inject your unique brand of passion into whatever you are doing and others will follow suit. You are influential this month and whatever tone you set will rub on others you come into contact with.

LOVE & RELATIONSHIPS - Taking the Lead
The Horse who takes the lead in any relationship will be completely irresistible this month! You have a totally addictive personality and can hold anyone captivated for hours. In fact they cannot get enough of you. Stay a little mysterious and you'll have anyone eating out of your hand. Enjoy yourself this month. Don't let any relationship get too heavy. Keep your sense of humor with everything and you'll have a ball of a time. The married Horse will also enjoy home life a whole lot more, with the brilliant white star dominating the chart. Also a fabulous month for getting married, getting engaged, starting a family or having a new baby.

EDUCATION - Try Something New
This is an exciting month for the young horse with many new things to experience and to try your hand at. Don't waste any opportunities that come your way to try something new. They may not come again; and they could lead to a whole new world opening up for you.

CHAPTER 5: ANALYSING YOUR LUCK IN EACH MONTH

TENTH MONTH
Nov 7th - Dec 6th 2012

BACK ON TRACK ONCE AGAIN AS EVERYTHING GOES RIGHT

Completion luck characterizes the month, bringing things you have been working on to a successful close. Projects get completed and new ones started. This is a fast-paced month when things happen quickly. You hardly have time to stop and think. Blink and you'll miss something. But this is exactly what makes you feel right at home! You are a free spirit and cannot stay in one place doing the same thing for too long. The coming month gives you plenty of variety and many opportunities to try new things. New people enter your life with the chance to make some great new friends. Seize every new experience with both hands and you'll come out of the month feeling extremely happy and satisfied with yourself.

WORK & CAREER - Going Well

Your career goes well, mainly because of your knack of striking up a good rapport with just about everyone you work with. You may have to juggle your responsibilities and even get someone to fill in for you, but working on slightly more flexible hours is acceptable if you keep producing the results. For those of you with sales targets to meet, start working on them early in the month; you could find that not only do you meet them early, you could seriously outperform yourself. Not a bad thing at year end when appraisals are made and promotions are conferred.

BUSINESS - Auspicious Times

Things are moving along at a speedy pace. Exciting times indeed for the Horse in business. If you've been looking for a good time to launch a new product or new initiative, this is the time. You have success and completion luck on your side and are able to project your enthusiasm onto others. Whether you're dealing with the client or the media, your exhilaration is infectious and will deliver the results you are looking for.

You also work as part of a team right now, so you should have no qualms including more team members into your fold. Also a promising time to look for possible new hires. Wear the **100 bird scarf** or display the **100 birds as a painting** in the office to attract exciting new opportunities.

LOVE & RELATIONSHIPS - Hidden Passion

Fire energy burns bright in your chart indicating a hidden passion surfacing at this time of your life. If you succumb to your desires, it could bring you either a lot of happiness or a lot of trouble you don't need. Be careful who you go after when it comes to romantic liaisons. Avoid illicit affairs because the headache and heartache that comes with it is not worth it at a time when the rest of your life is going so well. Love is definitely in the air; just control your passion and restrict it to good, clean fun. Married Horses meanwhile enjoy rediscovering each other.

EDUCATION - Scheduling Clashes

A month chock full of activities awaits the young Horse. You may be pulled in many different directions with your enthusiasm to try many different things. This may force you to pick what you want to pursue, which would be a shame because your capacity to learn new things right now is so great. It might be worth making the effort to make some scheduling changes, or to look for some other way around it.

ELEVENTH MONTH
Dec 7th - Jan 5th 2013

EXTREMELY AUSPICIOUS MONTH
What a lucky month indeed for the Horse! Your efforts from the year come together culminating in sweet success and good fortune. You enjoy wealth and prosperity luck, and for some of you, this could mean a windfall or bonus of some kind. You're in no shortage of money so you can afford to indulge yourself and your loved ones a little (or a lot). Enjoy the end-of-year festivities and make the most of any opportunities to network. You're in your element when it comes to making new friends, and having a few more could prove useful (and enjoyable) later on.

WORK & CAREER - Be Proactive
Your happy and relaxed attitude helps create a positive impression on others, boosting your popularity at the workplace. Others feel secure in commending your good work as you're productive without appearing threatening. Continue to spend as much time cultivating friendships with your colleagues as with your boss if you want things to stay this pleasant. But for those of you vying for a promotion, don't

waste time loitering around in the background. You may have to raise your game a be a little more aggressive, especially if you work in a competitive environment. Be proactive in volunteering yourself to take on more tasks. Show how reliable you can be. And stay out of any office politics that may arise. Display the **Monkey atop a Horse** on your work desk to boost promotion luck for you this month.

BUSINESS - A Promising Month

Wealth and prosperity luck is promising and you could stumble upon an opportunity to make some serious money. Don't be afraid to take some risks. You can afford to be daring in your decisions this month. If your gut feel tells you something is worth pursuing, maybe it is. You have spot-on instincts, so if you feel strongly enough about something, you don't really need numbers to back your decision up. A back-of-the envelope calculation should be good enough.

Sometimes business calls for on-the-spot decisions. Your horoscope luck says that this month you can afford to make some of these decisions purely on instinct. The next four weeks are happy ones for the entrepreneur Horse. For those of you are thinking of going into business with another party, make sure you stay in charge. Things work out better that way.

LOVE & RELATIONSHIPS - Communicate

Your key to happiness in love this month lies in good communication. Make time to supplement the physical with the emotional. **Romance blossoms** for the Horse from good heart-to-hearts with your partner. For the married Horse, do book yourselves a **romantic dinner** for two. The single Horse in the dating game can also look forward to a highly enjoyable month ahead. Your easy-going attitude makes you an engaging dinner partner and will earn you points if you're hoping to take the relationship to the next level. Stay relaxed and don't covet anything to the point where you become too easy. Stay a little mysterious and leave some things to the imagination and you will be simply irresistible.

CHAPTER 5: ANALYSING YOUR LUCK IN EACH MONTH

TWELVETH MONTH
Jan 6th - Feb 3rd 2013

BE CAREFUL AS YOU COULD GET ROBBED OR CHEATED

Tread carefully as there is risk of violence and loss. The aggressive number 7 surfaces again, bringing danger of robbery and betrayal. Don't trust others too easily, even if you think you know them. You could be let down even by those you consider friends. The thing is the betrayals you encounter may not even be intentional, so don't hold a grudge. Just keep your guard up so you minimize your losses. Step up security to the home this month and remember to check the doors are locked and secure at night. You can never be too careful about these things. Horses in business risk being taken for a ride. Be careful with smooth talkers and new acquaintances in your life that seem just a little too slick. Carry a talisman for protection. It is also a good idea to sleep with a **Lock Coin** under your pillow or mattress to keep your wealth safe this month.

Carry the Lock Coin or sleep with it under your pillow to avoid large losses and to counter the Robbery and Loss Star this month.

WORK & CAREER - Stay Alert

It is important to stay alert this month. Mistakes and slip-ups occur easily, so do counter check your work and be more careful. Those of you in competitive careers could see more rivals surfacing, making the workplace a sometimes unfriendly place. Don't let politics at the workplace get you down, but don't be naïve to it either. Stake your claim in your territory. You work better with others of the same gender this month. Don't let romantic issues cloud the picture when it comes to office romances. In fact, steer well clear of them – they do not bring good news. Your luck has taken a definite downturn so it is wise to stay careful. A misstep on your part could have dire consequences.

BUSINESS - Some Strong Competition

Competition heats up and you're going to have to use your cleverness to stay ahead of the competition this month. Some of your rivals could employ some non-sporting tactics. Be vigilant to what is going on and be ready to retaliate. Keep a tight rein on your finances and don't enter any deals without considering everything carefully. This is not a good time to enter into new ventures or sign anything with outsiders. Wait until next month when your luck improves. There is risk of money loss. Hold on big investments and limit your exposure to risk. This is a time when paying attention to detail pays off. Some misunderstandings may arise with business partners or associates due to the negative combination in your chart. If you have to extricate yourself from a partnership, wait till the afflictions in your chart clears next month before finalizing anything. This is a month to lie low and to stay low profile.

LOVE & RELATIONSHIPS - Complicated

Your love life could get a little complicated. You could find yourself in the middle of a love triangle you didn't plan. Don't play with fire when it comes to matters of the heart. Even if you don't view minor infidelities seriously, the other parties involved may; and this could end in violence.

Those of you who are married may have to deal with third party interference to the marriage. Even if nothing happened, rumors that get started could put a lot of strain on the marriage. You need to stay strong if you're going to come out of this unscathed. It is a good idea to wear the **anti-infidelity amulet** this month.

Chapter Six
PROTECTING YOUR TRINITY OF LUCK USING SPIRITUAL FENG SHUI

In recent years, the need to incorporate the vital Third Dimension into the practice of feng shui has become increasingly urgent - as we observe the unbalanced energies of the world erupt in earthquakes, giant tsunamis, volcanic explosions, fierce winds, snowstorms and raging forest fires. It seems as if the four elements of the cosmic environment which control the forces of Nature are taking turns to unleash their fearsome wrath on the world, in the process also generating fierce emotions of anger and desperation that elicit killing violence. Last year, the threat of nuclear radiation poisoning the world's atmosphere, its winds and waters also became potentially a fearsome reality. The world watched as Japan suffered - it was a big wakeup call!

CHAPTER 6 : PROTECTING YOUR TRINITY OF LUCK

Then came the hundreds of tornadoes unleashed on American States that destroyed towns and cities. Then came the fires that ravaged Arizona… Will 2012 see an end to nature's wrath?

So what are the four elements of the cosmic environment? These are fire and water, earth and wind. These four elements signify the cosmic forces of the Third Dimension in feng shui; these forces are powerful but they are not caused by some evil being out to wreak revenge or death on the inhabitants of the world.

What they are, are highly visual manifestations of the severe imbalances of energy that need to be righted, and the process of rebalancing causes millions of litres of water to get displaced, hence the severe rainfalls and the tsunamis. They cause thousands of miles of earth to get shifted, hence earthquakes and volcanic eruptions, which in turn causes winds in the upper atmosphere and the currents of the seas to go awry. Temperatures blow very hot and very cold… and pockets of the world's population experience suffering, loss and depravation!

In 2010 and 2011, the onslaught of natural and manmade disasters befalling the world were reflected in the feng shui and destiny charts of those years, and the revelations of the charts of 2012 suggest a need to use Spiritual Feng Shui to find solutions, seek safeguards and use protection to navigate through these turbulent years; to be prepared… so to speak.

In their great wisdom, the ancient Masters had somehow devised specific methods, rituals and almost magical ways to safely live through disastrous times. For of course these natural calamities have repeated themselves - in a series of cyclical patterns - over thousands of years. We know that the world's energies work in repeating patterns and that there are cycles of change which affect our wellbeing.

To cope with these dangerous forces, it is necessary to decipher the charts, analyze the destructive forces revealed in the patterns of annual elements and then to apply cosmic remedies and transcendental cures - all part of the Third Dimension that completes our practice of feng shui. To enhance our trinity of luck i.e. our Heaven, Earth and Mankind luck.

CHAPTER 6 : PROTECTING YOUR TRINITY OF LUCK

In practicing spiritual feng shui, we look to generate good mankind luck, the luck we directly create for ourselves. The Buddhists and the Hindus call this luck generating good KARMA… and this is a concept that can be found in many of the world's spiritual practices.

Karma suggests that we can improve our luck, increase our longevity and experience happiness by purifying karmic debts and creating good merit through the practice of kindness, compassion and generosity. These are the basics. Thus we discovered through the years that our feng shui work and advice always worked best when we mindfully input genuinely kind motivations.

This led us to start using rituals of purification and appeasement to keep the four elements of fire, water, earth and wind balanced around our places of living and working. We discovered that there were direct correlations between the four elements of the cosmic world and the five elements of the human world.

Different animal signs are ruled by different elements at different times. Here we found that in time dimension feng shui - analyzing the annual and monthly charts to study the movement of element energy over time-spiritual methods played a big part in helping us improve our use of purification rituals. They helped us to bridge the divide between the cosmic worlds - the spiritual worlds that existed alongside ours, and to add so much to our practice of feng shui. Included in the practice of Third Dimension spiritual feng shui are rituals and vocal incantations that can quell imbalances of energy.

There are powerful prayers and special offerings that can be used to invoke the aid of the cosmic beings of our space, the local landlords who rule our environment; the spirits and protectors who can assist us subdue the angry earth, control the raging waters, and basically keep us safe, making sure we will not be in the wrong place at the wrong time, that somehow we will change our plans, delay our travels or just stay home during crucial times when the elements of the world will be out of sync and raging.

Spiritual feng shui brings the practice of feng shui into other realms of existence. It addresses parallel worlds that exist alongside ours; cosmic worlds inhabited by beings we call Spirits, local Landlords, protectors or even Deities who have supremacy over the elements.

CHAPTER 6 : PROTECTING YOUR TRINITY OF LUCK

There are Earth Deities and Wind Deities, Water and Fire Gods - in the old lineage texts of the ancient masters, references are made to the Four Direction Guardians, the heavenly kings who protect the four directions, North, South, East and West corners of our world, of the Eight Direction Goddesses who subdue destructive forces of wind and water and protect mankind.

Much of the information related to these powerful cosmic Deities has become the stuff of legends but they are real; and it is not difficult to invoke the assistance of these cosmic beings. It would be a big mistake to dismiss them as mere superstition!

Included here are some of the easier methods of spiritual feng shui which just about anyone can indulge in without compromising your belief systems. Always perform these practices with good motivation which is to keep your family safe, and your life humming along without success blocking obstacles.

You will notice that the use of symbolism activated by the mind's concentrated power is extremely potent, as are the purifying and offering rituals. One of the most effective way of staying safe and secure in your world is to make and wear special magic diagrams that incorporate sacred symbols and incantations or mantras into what we collectively refer to as amulets.

This practice is usually referred to as transcendental feng shui and the methods are shamanic, totally magical in their effect. The amulet can be customized to benefit different animal signs directly, incorporating the energizing symbols and syllables most beneficial to their elements in any given year. The amulet for the Horse is given in this chapter here.

Spiritual feng shui also involves identifying the special Deity who has the greatest affinity with specific animal signs - these can be viewed as your Guardian Bodhisattva, similar to the patron saint or spiritual guide of each animal sign.

When you invite your Guardian Bodhisattva into your home, make offerings and recite their relevant mantra, you will benefit from the full force of their protective power. They will not only ensure that you stay safe and protected but will also multiply the potency of your time and space feng shui updates as well.

Incense Offerings to Appease Local Spirit Protectors

Everyone benefits from learning how to make incense offerings on a regular basis to communicate directly with the "local landlords" that reside alongside us in our home space, on our street, in our town or village or sometimes on separate floors of high rise buildings. There is no need to be scared of them or to fear them. Most will leave human tenants alone.

When incense is offered to them, it creates the element of gratitude on their part; that is when they could assist you in whatever requests you make. It is not a widely known fact, but Spirit beings of the cosmic realm are always hungry, and at their lowest levels, they are known as hungry ghosts. The problem is that they are unable to eat! They cannot swallow food as their necks are said to be extremely narrow and the only way they can appease their hunger is by smelling aromatic, pungent incense which is yummy to them.

But just burning the incense alone is not as effective as reciting 21 times the blessing incantation that transforms the incense into sustenance for them, and then it is like giving them a feast, and the stronger the scent is, the tastier it will be to them.

CHAPTER 6 : **PROTECTING YOUR TRINITY OF LUCK**

There are so many auspicious benefits to preparing and then burning this incense offering in the outside space of your home, and also in the inside space by moving round each room three times in a clockwise direction.

Done once a week on your *Day of Obstacles*, the incense will chase out all negativities and cleanse your home of bad energy. The local spirits will then also attract success, good health and wellbeing. Whatever disharmony there is in the home will quickly dissolve and all the afflictions of the year will also dissipate.

For the Horse person, the best day to perform this incense offering ritual is **every Wednesday**. And the best time would be to do it anytime between **1 p.m. to 3 p.m.** in the afternoon.

Offering incense is one of the best ways to appease the local spirits of the land.

CHAPTER 6 : PROTECTING YOUR TRINITY OF LUCK

In the old days, practitioners of this ritual would burn freshly-cut juniper on hot charcoal and this gives off a very pleasant aroma together with white smoke which is also very pleasing to the spirits. This method continues to be used by the mountain people such as the *Sherpas* of the Himalayan mountain regions.

In fact, if you go trekking in Nepal, you will see all along the trekking routes examples of these incense offering rituals which are done to appease the local protectors hence keeping both visiting trekkers as well as the local people safe.

It is said that the more undeveloped a place is, the greater the presence of local spirits. Mountainous places are great favorites with the beings of the cosmic world. This is why those who go mountain climbing should always wear amulets to keep them safe from being harmed by some naughty wandering spirits.

Today however, especially if you live in the city, it is more convenient to use specially formulated incense pellets which burn easily and which give off a beautiful pungent aroma. The Malays and the Indians in Malaysia call this *kemenyen* and the Chinese sometimes use sandalwood incense powder to achieve the same effect.

Use a special incense burner that comes with a handle and as you light the incense recite prayers that consecrate the incense so that it becomes easier for the spirits to enjoy the offering incense. Remember to take a humble attitude when making the offering, and if you are a Buddhist, you can also take refuge in the triple gems before you start. The incantation mantra, to be recited at least 21 times is:

NAMAH SARVA TATHAGATA AVALOKITE OM SAMBHARA SAMBHARA HUNG

Then think that you are making offering of the incense to the landlords and protectors of your house, your street and your neighborhood. You can think that they are accepting the incense and then you can request for specific illness or obstacles to be removed.

Those born in the year of the Horse can request for protection in 2012 when they are feeling weak or lacking in energy.

CHAPTER 6 : **PROTECTING YOUR TRINITY OF LUCK**

Customized Cosmic Amulet to Strengthen Victory Luck for the Horse

There is a group of 102 Protective Amulets, reportedly first made in the Tibetan Nyingma monastery of Samye, the monastery in Tibet founded by the powerful Tibetan Lotus Born Buddha known as Guru Padmasambhava or Guru Rinpoche that is designed according to astrological calculations using the Chinese calendar i.e. based on the 60 year cycle of 12 animal signs and 5 elements.

Feng shui astrology attributes different influences arising from the different combinations that occur between the 12 animals and the 5 elements each year; these combinations of influences reveal the nuances of good and bad luck according to the year of birth.

Every sign requires different sanskrit syllables, symbols and invocations, which are meant to subdue bad influences facing the sign.

The amulet that is customized to the animal sign also simultaneously promotes all-round good influences to come your way; it protects your property, business and work interests, and your family and your loved ones.

Amulet of the Wood Element

The Horse benefits from wearing what is referred to as the Wood amulet; and it is shared with the other "Fire Sign" of the Zodiac, the Snake. The amulet is usually drawn as a circle and it incorporates the empowering dependent arising mantra. The outermost circle is embellished with designs of the Wood and sometimes also the Fire symbol.

The amulet is usually drawn as a circle sometimes signifying the underbelly of a protective tortoise. To the Tibetans, the tortoise signifies the protector of the Universe. The centre of the circle is inscribed with invocations of safety and protection around which is an eight petal lotus with more protective supplications.

The Horse belongs to the Fire element, so Wood energy will strengthen its intrinsic element. It should be written in red cinnamon ink and on dark red or yellow paper, or silk, and then folded, then kept in a suitable casing and worn near to the body.

CHAPTER 6 : PROTECTING YOUR TRINITY OF LUCK

The Horse benefits from the Wood Amulet. Just having this amulet near you will suppress any negative afflictions or influences that threaten to harm you.

Worn touching the body, especially if the amulet has been suitably consecrated, it can block off all adverse forces and keep planetary afflictions subdued. The amulet for the Horse can be made of paper or silk and then kept inside a leather or metal pouch. In 2012, Metal element signifies power and influence, so having a gold or silver casing is appropriate.

We have also incorporated other amulets onto silk neck scarves that are beneficial for the Horse. These are suitable for dressing up your outfit while it watches over you at the same time. Most amulets have a series of three concentric circles of mantras with an eight petalled lotus in the centre.

The Horse can also wear auspicious wishfulfilling amulets as well those with the mantra of the Goddess Tara or with the special mantra that fulfils all your wishes:

OM PADMO USHNISHA BIMALE HUM PEH

And because the Horse enjoys the luck of victorious attainments it is extremely beneficial for Horse to cement this year's good fortune vibes by inviting the **wishfulfilling jewel** into the home as well.

Clear Crystal Ball with Ru Yi to Enhance Recognition Luck

The Horse sign has good fortune stars in 2012 and what it needs to actualize the potential of victorious good fortune is to strengthen its Power Luck. This is best done with the symbol of the Ru Yi and because Earth energy in 2012 stands for wealth and financial success luck, it is extremely beneficial to display a clear crystal ball that is solid with the Golden Ru Yi embedded within.

This is a very worthwhile new addition to your home and it is best placed in the South corner of your coffee table in the living room. This benefits the Horse sign's luck. You can also place it on your office or work desk.

A clear crystal ball with Ru Yi embedded brings attainment luck for the Horse this year.

Wish Granting Tree to Attract Serious Prosperity Luck

The 2012 paht chee chart reveals the presence of one pillar where the elements are in a productive relationship. The month pillar shows yang Water producing yang Wood, and with the presence of the lap chun in this year's calendar, it means that there will be rejuvenated productive energy during the year. This will bring about excellent new growth.

CHAPTER 6 : **PROTECTING YOUR TRINITY OF LUCK**

To activate this, it is very beneficial to display a young tree of wealth that is in full bloom and which also represents a new beginning so a tree that is usually associated with the season of Spring is quite ideal. This is a feng shui enhancing symbol that is suitable for everyone.

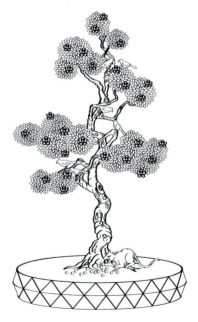

Display a tree of wealth in full bloom for powerful growth and renewal luck this year.

Golden Wealth Wheel for Wealth Creation

To increase your store of prosperity luck, the Horse can display the spinning magical wealth wheel which is created from two circular brass plates that are inscribed with the powerful mandalas of the male and female wealth Gods of the cosmic traditions. Each side has eight images within the eight petals of a stylised lotus.

These images of wealth gods and goddesses are placed facing each other, and when the plates are turned, the energy released from the wealth Deities being pleased attracts great wealth and prosperity into the home or office.

At the back of the Male deities are the eight auspicious signs and in the centre the seed syllable Hum; behind the female deities are the royal emblems and in the centre the seed syllable Hrih.

Do take note that this is a sacred representation of the Wealth Deities bringing wealth. It is an excellent idea to spin this Golden Wealth Wheel at least once a day. Do place the wheel on a high level i.e. on a sideboard rather than on a low coffee table.

Plaque of a Single Victory Horse

Those born in the Horse year can truly benefit if they activate the excellent Victory Horse. This strengthens the attainment aspects of their lucky energy in 2012. This year, the flying star numbers indicate that the Horse is blessed by the white number 1, which is the Victory number.

So the Horse location of the South in the feng shui chart is governed by the number 1. Activating with the image or plaque of a single Victory Horse brings the luck of winning and of attainments.

Fire Totem Talisman Pendant to Safeguard Long Term Prospects

One of the most popular ways of wearing several auspicious cosmic symbols together is to use the totem concept which groups three or more powerful instruments or symbols stacked one on top of another. Totems make powerful talismans when they are correctly made and properly energized with special incantations.

Cosmic totems that put together element groups of protective sacred symbols can be excellent for compensating for a vital missing element. In 2012,

CHAPTER 6 : PROTECTING YOUR TRINITY OF LUCK

the Fire element signified by the color red is required to bring about a proper balance to the energies of the world; but more than that, 2012 is the kind of year when it is extremely beneficial to invoke the powerful Bodhisattva and deity guardians of the Earth, many of whom are associated with sanskrit syllables.

The **Fire Totem Talisman**

comprises three powerful sanskrit syllables - at the base is Bam, followed by Ah, and then Hrih at the top. These syllables are strongly associated with the Tibetan spiritual traditions and the shamans of pre-Buddhist Tibet wear these syllables to keep them safe and empowered at all times. But these syllables are also used as wish-granting aids in powerful spiritual visualisations. The syllable *Hrih* is a very powerful symbol which protects and also sends out a great deal of loving energy. It makes the wearer appear softer, warmer and kinder. The Fire Totem Talisman is a pendant made completely of gold which can be worn touching the throat chakra. Not many know it but the throat chakra is red in color and it governs the power of one's speech.

> Anyone wanting their spoken words, their speech, their selling proposals and so on to become empowered can wear this totem pendant.

If you work in a profession where the way you talk, give a speech, make a proposal and otherwise use your voice is crucial, then this totem pendant is ideal for you. Those in the teaching profession, in law and in the entertainment industry, for instance, would benefit greatly from wearing it.

There is a lotus and an utpala flower joining these seed syllables - and all the five items in the totem are related to the Fire energy of red. The color red signifies the Fire element. The lotus signifies purity and the utpala flower suggests the attainment of great wisdom. This is a very powerful emblem not just for protection but more importantly for empowerment. When you wear them, think that they exude rays of red light radiating outwards from you in all directions.

Rising Blue Dragon to Activate the Year's Heaven Luck

The year's chart also reveals the importance of tapping effectively into the year's beautiful and much-needed heaven luck. The centre of the feng shui chart is

CHAPTER 6 : PROTECTING YOUR TRINITY OF LUCK

governed by the number 6 which apart from being an auspicious white number, is also representative of Big Metal and signifies an abundance of heaven luck. Activating heaven luck not only attracts power and influence into your life, but good fortune luck also comes unexpectedly.

Heaven luck is an important component of the trinity of luck and in 2012 harvesting the year's store of heaven luck energy is what will boost your feng shui luck. The way to do this is to simulate the mighty Water Dragon of the year looking upwards into the skies getting ready to fly into a clear blue sky with the sunshine sending rays of yang chi all round. Displayed on a sideboard in the centre of the home, this taps into the powerful energy of the Dragon.

Place the Rising Blue Dragon in the center of the living room for fabulous heaven luck in this Year of the Water Dragon.

Invoking Horse's Guardian Bodhisattva Mahasthama Prapta

The Horse's Bodhisattva Guardian is Mahasthama Prapta whose presence in your home or in your work space can be most beneficial. Look for an image that "speaks" to you and then invite the image into your home. Just having his presence in the home is symbolically powerful especially if placed in the South, the Horse's home location.

Place offerings of water bowls, candles and food to establish a "connection" and each time you make incense offering to the local landlords and environmental spirits, do include your Guardian Deity by name in your list of recipients. It is a good idea to make the dedication to to your Guardian Deity first.

This does not need to be a very elaborate or special ritual. The key to success in incorporating spiritual feng shui into your daily life is to be very relaxed, confident and joyous about all that you do. What is so beneficial about having your Guardian Deity in your home is that the surrounding spirits of the cosmic world always respect the Bodhisattvas and Buddhas, and when you invoke their protection, it offers you safe refuge from being harmed by the spirits that may be residing in your space.

So What Do You Think?

We hope you enjoyed this book and gained some meaningful insights about your own personal horoscope and animal sign. This book, if used properly and regularly, is a goldmine of feng shui knowledge… so hopefully you are already feeling a difference and enjoying the results of positive actions you have taken.

But Don't Stop Now!

You can receive the latest weekly news and even more feng shui updates from Lillian herself absolutely FREE! Learn even more of her secrets and open your mind to the deeper possibilities of feng shui today.

Lillian Too's FREE online weekly ezine is now AVAILABLE!

Here's how easy it is to subscribe. Just go online to: *www.lilliantoomandalaezine.com* and sign up today!

Your newsletter will be delivered automatically
to your inbox each week
....

You will receive a special FREE BONUS from Lillian when
you subscribe to Lillian's FREE Mandala Weekly Ezine…
but it's only available to those who register online at:
www.lilliantoomandalaezine.com
....

Once you register for the weekly newsletter,
you become eligible for special discounts and offers only
available to ezine subscribers!
....

DON'T BE LEFT OUT! JOIN TODAY!

Thanks again for investing in yourself and in this book.
Now join me online every week and learn how easy it really
is to make good feng shui a way of life!

Lillian's online FREE weekly ezine is only available when
you register online at *www.lilliantoomandalaezine.com*